RIFFS & MEANING

MANIC STREET PREACHERS AND *KNOW YOUR ENEMY*

Stephen Lee Naish

HEADPRESS

# CONTENTS

*For Jamie*

RIFFS & MEANING

MANIC STREET PREACHERS AND *KNOW YOUR ENEMY*

Stephen Lee Naish

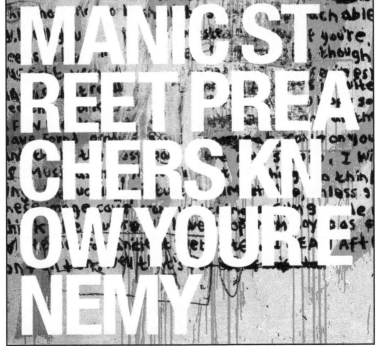

# INTRODUCTION

The musical notes are only five in number
but their melodies are so numerous
that one cannot hear them all.
　　—Sun Tzu, *The Art of War*

THE LAST SONG I HEARD AS THE WORLD SAID GOODBYE TO
the twentieth century was Motorcycle Emptiness by the Manic
Street Preachers. I was jammed into Cardiff's Millennium
Stadium along with 57,000 complete strangers. Over a million
more viewers worldwide had joined in as the performance was
broadcast live across the globe on the BBC. It was a massive
event, and the knowledge that so many had either turned up
or tuned in was an extraordinary thing to realize. It was fitting
that this song played out the closing moments of the century.

Motorcycle Emptiness summed up an era of perplexing
narratives and outcomes: intense global warfare, political
brinkmanship, American cultural and militaristic supremacy,
and the ideologies of fascism, communism, democracy, and
capitalism all fighting it out for dominance. The downward
trajectory of late twentieth-century mankind was all but
encapsulated within the yearning verses and jubilant chorus
of Motorcycle Emptiness. Yet locked within that gigantic
rugby arena with no recognizable faces around me (my
friends were long lost to the crowds), the world could have
ended as the prophecies had foreseen and I'd have accepted

it without resistance. It was a perfect way to go quietly into the night, or headfirst into oblivion. But the world didn't end (obviously), and a few moments after the bells had tolled for a new century, the handsome form of Manic Street Preachers' vocalist and guitarist James Dean Bradfield strolled back out on-stage with an acoustic guitar slung under his arm and began strumming the opening chords to Frankie Valli's 1967 hit Can't Take My Eyes Off You. If Motorcycle Emptiness had been the final curtain call of the twentieth century, and was loaded with significance, then Can't Take My Eyes Off You was its flipside. The dawning of a new era was utterly irrelevant, yet also brilliant. And here lies the contradiction of the Manic Street Preachers: a socialist rock band from the Welsh valleys whose every song lyric is steeped in class politics, capitalist critique, historical significance, and personal circumstance, yet they are and have always been exquisite entertainers, well attuned to the ridiculous pomp and irreverence of rock 'n' roll theatrics.

I'll admit here that I am not a Manic Street Preachers purist. My earliest encounter was sometime in the early nineties via my older sister's cassette copy of the band's second album *Gold Against the Soul* (1993), and whilst I approved of heavier tracks like Sleepflower and From Despair To Where I could barely get past the loose funk of the record's third track La Tristesse Durera. I was an Americanized hard rock kid living in the suburbs of Leicester in the UK, and anything softer than Metallica's One was discredited in an instant as whiney slush. In the early 1990s I morphed into a teenage grunger, with long greasy hair, tie-dye t-shirt, and steel-toed boots. If the message wasn't delivered earnestly by a longhaired growler in a plaid shirt and Doc Martens boots then I wasn't listening. Then around 1995, I got a natty haircut, found some of my dad's old Fred Perry polo shirts and rocked the indie kid look of Oasis' Gallagher brothers, Blur's Damon Albarn, and then the Manic Street Preachers as they were in 1996, a mix of Topshop casual and Debenhams glam. I've surfed along the surface of these three distinct musical movements ever since.

However, whilst I shifted personas and styles so did the Manic Street Preachers. They had started out in the late-eighties as eyeliner-clad politicized punk rockers. Tight white jeans and stenciled slogans sprayed across their mothers' blouses that read things like 'All rock 'n' roll is Homosexual' and 'Terminal Young Thing'. With their 1992 debut album *Generation Terrorists* they announced they would become instantly famous, sell sixteen million records, play Wembley Stadium (the benchmark of success) and then split up in "mess of eyeliner and spray-paint". This would be a grandly artistic, yet also nihilistic gesture. Musically, the band mixed The Clash with Guns N' Roses with their sharp political lyricism borrowed from Public Enemy's critical stylistics. They crammed each of their songs with high impact cultural cues that brimmed with fury and intelligence.

The band's upbringing was deeply working class and rooted in strong socialist ideals that resonated from the 1984/5 strikes that shook the mining community of Blackwood, Wales, from which the band originated. Their second album, the aforementioned *Gold Against the Soul*, was a straight-ahead and sober hard rock affair. Songs like From Despair To Where, Life Becoming A Landslide and Yourself fell into MTV's *Headbangers Ball*-endorsed outlook of rocking riffs, heavy drums, and growling vocals. Yet the lyrical content of *Gold Against the Soul* dealt with a sensitivity that would have made most metalheads puke. The aesthetics changed too, the eyeliner, feather boas, and stenciled shirts were decommissioned, and in their place a more subtle attire of pinstriped suits, designer brands, mature facial stubble and gentleman hats prevailed. But this incarnation would not last for very long.

The band's monolithic third record *The Holy Bible* (1994) saw them once again dramatically shift styles. The sound was compressed, apocalyptic postpunk, matched with vicious polemic style lyrics and a militaristic aesthetic of mismatched sailor suits and camouflage attire. Songs such as Faster, PCP and Revol sounded like nothing else at the time. But tragedy struck. The band's chief lyricist and rhythm guitarist Richey James Edwards vanished just prior to a brief trip to America to promote *The Holy Bible*.

And this is where my own fandom begins. I am one of those so-called 'new' fans that the Manic Street Preachers raked up as they returned in 1996 as a three-piece and embraced a more accessible sound and style. Their first 'post Edwards' album, *Everything Must Go* (1996), took until the record's fourth single Australia to work its magic on me. When I brought a copy of the record from the local HMV, it didn't leave my CD player for six months. It was only replaced by copies of *Generation Terrorists* and *The Holy Bible*. *Gold Against the Soul* made a short reappearance on the player and this time I gave it the full hearing.

From this point onwards a large portion of my life was devoted to being a follower/fanatic of the Manic Street Preachers. It has not just been the consumption of their albums, singles, music videos, interviews, and live performances that has taken up so much of my time but the countless cultural, political, literary, philosophical, and historical reference points and quotations that have littered the band's lyrics and adorned their record covers. The lyrical content of a Manic

Street Preachers song is akin to a found collection of footnotes and citations in which the main body of the thesis has been ripped out. Using these footnotes, it requires the listener to seek out the original source material and piece together the main text and build the narrative back up from scratch. A task that might appear arduous at first, but in the theatre of rock 'n' roll, is an awesome pleasure to undertake.

Often the lyrics of a Manic Street Preachers record concoct an alternative narrative where the losers still lose the war but the battles rage on internally. For example, the first single from the band's fifth album *This is My Truth Tell Me Yours* (1998), the grandiose and epic If You Tolerate This Your Children Will Be Next contained a lyric that detailed the ragtag band of Welsh farmers who took up arms and joined with the International Brigade to fight against fascism in the 1936–39 Spanish Civil War. After absorbing the song's lyrics and reading interviews the band gave around the time of the single's release, I felt obligated to discover more about this aspect of twentieth century history and why the band felt that this conflict from another country and another time was worthy of bringing to the attention of a contemporary mainstream audience. When I discovered that writers such as George Orwell and Ernest Hemingway had documented their personal experiences of the war in *Homage to Catalonia* and *For Whom the Bell Tolls* respectively, it only added to the romanticism of that conflict and the nobility of those who selflessly fought in it. Of course, the victors of the war were still Francisco Franco's Falangists. A totalitarian fascist dictatorship was installed and reigned until Franco's death in 1975. The song was a clarion call about history repeating itself. Thus, a sunny holiday destination from when I was kid was revealed as a complex and fraught society of survivors with a living memory of dictatorship.

*Everything Must Go* and *This is My Truth...* made Manic Street Preachers one of Britain's biggest bands of the 1990s. When they returned in 2001 and launched their sixth album *Know Your Enemy* in the communist hotbed of Cuba, I was immediately drawn to the audacious history of the small island that had resisted American cultural and political imperialism. I investigated Fidel Castro's Cuban Revolution and Che Guevara's earlier jaunt of discovery across South America that he'd documented in *The Motorcycle Diaries*. A land crucified as a socialist backwater, and a place that might be considered a relic of history, was introduced to me by a band discussing their desire to play to a nation that has globally been left behind by the American embargo imposed upon it in 1960. Old scholarly reports, hardboiled Cold War thrillers, and Castro's own dry but compelling 2008 autobiography, *My Life*, were greedily consumed in order to fully grasp the details.

Manic Street Preachers shone a light on figures and historical events that were mere annotations in the triumphalism of the neoliberal age. Through quotations on record sleeves to name dropping them in song, the band have restored or reassessed cultural figures such as Paul Robeson, Valerie Solanas, Kevin Carter, Sylvia Plath, Jean-Paul Sartre, Dennis Potter, Karl Marx, Harold Pinter, Albert Camus, Octave Mirbeau, Chuck D, Vladimir Lenin, and Richard Nixon, back into the popular discourse. It is important that these figures remain in the cultural lexicon, because, let's face it, we need them. We need to learn from their mistakes, and we need to revel in their victories. Their voices, the words they wrote, the actions they took, the lives they lived were often against the grain of what is perceived as the established order. Even if they failed to live it out, they created an alternative, and a different understanding to everything. We need to understand that their failure is also ours. For it is us who have failed to take heed of the wisdom, the alternatives, and the warnings from history. This is a metaphor for the Manic Street Preachers themselves. A band that often placed themselves counter to the current trends in popular music and politics, but persisted with their version of events nonetheless.

And this is where *Know Your Enemy* comes in. As I'll discuss throughout this book, the album is so eccentric it sticks out as the untameable child of Manic Street Preachers' records. When asked by *Noisey* to rank his own records, James Dean Bradfield put it second from bottom (above the 2004 mishap *Lifeblood*) as his least favourite. Even he ultimately blamed the failure of *Lifeblood* on *Know Your Enemy*'s iconoclast ideals, stating that 'the malaise that led to *Lifeblood* was kind of *Know Your Enemy*'s fault because when we came in to do this album we were reacting to the massive success in Europe and other parts of the world.'[1]

The reasons for this general consensus towards *Know Your Enemy* are varied and will be explored further, but at a glance, the musical styles are diverse with no previous pointers, no set pattern or coherent path to guide the listener though. The politics of *Know Your Enemy* is messy, the band seemed to want to revive the vibrant mood and protest of *Generation Terrorists* and *The Holy Bible*, but the idealism of youth was absent. This leads to another point. The band members were indeed older; their reintegrated political idealism came across as stubborn and grouchy in interviews. Yet, despite all of this, I believe that *Know Your Enemy* holds more relevance and significance than fans, and even the band themselves, give it credit for. *Know Your Enemy* is a critical album because it acts as a pivotal point to previous incarnations of the band and as an indicator towards their future as a band that for good or ill identify with leftist politics and continually reinvent themselves. *Know Your Enemy* was a requirement. It needed to be made, it needed to reference the past, yet also set the future in motion. Without it (and in some respects, *Lifeblood*) the reinvention and ambition seen on *Send Away the Tigers*, *Journal for Plague Lovers*, and *Futurology*, might not have existed.

Whilst some tracks on the record might not fall into what might be considered a 'classic Manics' category of anthems like Faster, Motorcycle Emptiness, Australia or Design For Life, the record was a genuine attempt by the band to explore new avenues in sound, embrace their base political views, reinvent themselves away from the shadow of Richey Edwards, renew their stance as music industry provocateurs, antagonize other bands, and basically be the band I, and many others, really wanted them to be at this point in their career. The record is as raw as the Manic Street Preachers had been in a long while. Not since their earliest Blackwood demos of the late 1980s recorded in James Dean Bradfield's parent's living room, or the scratchy bombast of the Heavenly Records era, have we had such a potent, instinctive and unrefined version of the band. After the polished sheen of *Everything Must Go* and *This is My Truth...* it is shocking, yet also exhilarating to hear the band impose a new set of rules upon themselves and endeavour to accomplish something entirely different to the band's past recordings.

I should disclose a short note on the following. The aim of this book is to treat the Manic Street Preachers as a singular entity, a commodity, in order to better understand their own failure to live up to the lofty ambitions they first placed upon themselves when they emerged in the early nineties. This has to happen for a number of reasons. Firstly, each member has a strong personality, and fans of the band, including myself, often fixate on these aspects and traits. This would be important if this was a straight-up biography of the band's career, but each path the band has taken that has led to either triumph or failure needs to be taken as a collective decision the band made. Each member also has a unique role within the band dynamic. Sean Moore and James Dean Bradfield have for the most part shouldered the music, whilst Nicky Wire and Richey Edwards managed the lyrics, and the visual aspects such as sleeve artwork and quotations. Again, every action in this respect needs to be seen in the context of a collective move. There are many elements that make up the Manic Street Preachers; I'm only concerned with the whole. So, in order to ascertain aspects of the band's politics, the musical directions they have taken, the aesthetics they have employed, and the lyrical themes of their songs, I have on occasion had to dispense with the individuals, not, I admit, a very fan friendly thing to do. Thus, unlike the comprehensive study, *Everything: A Book About Manic Street Preachers* by journalist, Simon Price, which chronicled the first decade of the band's existence, this book will not pull focus on James Dean Bradfield's brooding manliness and guitar heroics. It does not touch upon Richey Edwards' tortured genius and attempt to uncover the mysteries of his disappearance. I will not discuss Nicky Wire's obsession with domestic chores and vacuum cleaners, or submit to Sean Moore's obsession with the latest gadgets and, as discovered in the 2015 documentary film, *No Manifesto*, his love of firearms. The eccentric personal habits of the individual members of the Manic Street Preachers have been well documented in previous books, interviews, and documentary films.

In the last few years, the early history of the band has

faced immense coverage as the records from this era have been reissued as anniversary editions. *The Holy Bible* has had its own meticulous study in *Triptych: Three Studies of Manic Street Preachers' The Holy Bible* which brilliantly pulled apart that record and the time it was recorded in numerous and engaging angles. My concern here is not this era as such, but the moments afterwards as the band forged ahead in the new century as a three-piece band, aware of their history, but wanting to distance themselves from it. I want to focus on *Know Your Enemy* and uncover what it reveals about the later politics and ideals of the band, and why this brave, uncouth, and under-loved album deserves reconsideration as one of the band's finest endeavours. To paraphrase Greil Marcus' quotation that appears on the band's rarities compilation *Lipstick Traces: A Secret History of Manic Street Preachers,* what appeals to me about this era of the band's career are the gaps and the moments when the story that has lost its voice somehow recovers it. *Know Your Enemy* is an album about recovering a voice and recovering something that the band, and maybe even the fans, felt they had lost, as Bradfield remarked to *Noisey*: 'We thought that we had lost some of that original punk spirit that we'd had. It had kind of always been in the lyrics and some of our performances, but we thought we'd become too polished.'[2]

In order to fully comprehend the enormity of *Know Your Enemy* and its past and future repercussions we have to first understand how the band got there. What follows is a short version of the Manic Street Preachers history up until the point of *Know Your Enemy*. It is in no way comprehensive, that would now require several volumes. After this, I'll take a pause and reflect on *Know Your Enemy* from a number of different angles. Firstly, I'll delve into a track by track analysis and make connections with past and future recordings. I'll then discuss the band's trip to Cuba to launch *Know Your Enemy*, their meeting with Fidel Castro, and the press, and fan base reaction of the concert. I'll then examine the B-sides that appeared on the single releases from *Know Your Enemy*. This is necessary because whilst *Know Your Enemy* is a diverse mix, the singles that came from the record contained B-sides that also offered a great range of musical styles and themes that point back to the past and also towards the future. I'll use this chapter to make a case for the band's use of B-sides and extra tracks as a way of discovering new approaches and forging new directions on subsequent records. As *Know Your Enemy* had such a mixed review from critics and fans, I thought it was important to allow for some discussion from listeners. In this chapter, a number of Manic Street Preachers fans find merit in *Know Your Enemy*'s obtuse direction, but also a sense of trying to regain or relive past glories that may or may not have been wise to revisit. Once *Know Your Enemy* has been discussed in-depth, and its ideological points have been made, the band's narrative will then continue in the shadow of that record. As a conclusion, I'll discuss where I see *Know Your Enemy* in the grander scheme of the Manic Street Preachers' career, and why the band's politics have sometimes gelled with the popular mood, but also often grated.

# A SHORT HISTORY OF
# MANIC STREET PREACHERS

IN A DARKENED CORNER OF A SMALL BEDROOM IN THE rain-lashed town of Blackwood, South Wales, four adolescents, tucked under a blanket, whisper and snigger to themselves. A lone flashlight illuminates their shenanigans. They pass between themselves books and magazines, excited by the scandalous contents. At any moment a knock on the door could come, an offer of a cup of tea or a cheese sandwich could disturb their fumblings, their secrets discovered by disapproving parents. The books and magazines they rummage through are not the latest editions of porno magazines acquired from the local newsagents. Nor are they passages from erotic fiction classics like *Story of O*. The books are J.D. Salinger's *Catcher in the Rye*, Jack Kerouac's *On the Road*, S.E Hinton's *Rumble Fish*, and the magazines are the latest issues of music bibles, *Sounds*, *NME* and *Melody Maker*. What's happening under the covers isn't adolescent indulgence but a cultural education. The Manic Street Preachers were Manic Street Preachers years before they picked up guitars or wrote song lyrics. The real phase one of the band's incarnation was the accumulation of every facet of popular and literary culture and knowledge available to them in the sleepy backwaters of Blackwood. They knew it would be put to good use in the future, but at this point the means of production were absent.

In the mid 1980s, Thatcher launched an all-out assault on the British working classes by purging the mining industry and proclaiming that the collectivism of society was about as useful as an arse on an elbow. Thatcher wanted the costly pits closed and to increase reliance on imported fuels. The National Union of Miners, led by Arthur Scargill, voted to organise a national strike, and rise up in protest against the government initiative to close the mines. What was missing in this scenario was a sympathetic ear and solidarity from other unions such as the Trades Union Congress. Thatcher mobilized the Police Force from all over the UK to quash the rebellion and violent confrontation between picketers and police was common. After a year's stand-off, Thatcher and her cronies won the day, and the decimation was absolute:

> Thatcher continued her plan and the wider program of de-industrialisation in the name of the privileged minority. The majority, personified by the hopelessness of the destroyed mining communities, being left with unemployment, want, poverty and no chance for a happy, or peaceful existence.[3]

This sense of defeat infected great swaths of the industrial North and seeped into the daily existence of Blackwood. It was in this heady environment of class civil war, and its aftermath that the four teenage boys began gorging themselves on literature and popular culture. Quotations from the literary greats were considered just as important to rock star posturing in the weekly music magazines. It is no surprise that when the Manic Street Preachers launched themselves at the world they arrived almost fully formed as a brash class-conscious punk racket in stenciled slogan shirts, eyeliner and a neat line in quotable quips.

"I'm going down to Suicide Alley."
Suicide Alley single sleeve

Suicide Alley, in 1988, the first recording deemed professional by the Manic Street Preachers, was a brisk and shabby punker intended to strike up a rock 'n' roll revolution at a time when British music was dominated by fey indie, dream-pop, and hedonic acid house scene. At this point the charismatic Richey Edwards was not yet a member of the band, though he was responsible for taking Suicide Alley's cover photograph, showing the band hanging tough down a Blackwood back alley. The image was a recognizable homage to one of their chief influences, The Clash, and looked strikingly similar to the seminal punk band's 1977 debut record. Indeed, James Dean Bradfield, in an interview with *Ultimate Guitar* years later recalled that Suicide Alley:

> was recorded in a disused miner's institute in a place called Cwmfelinfach. I remember recording it in the basement of that disused miner's institute. I remember everything about it: I remember being nervous and trying to replicate something off a Clash record.[4]

It is incredible to think that an institution smashed by Thatcher's iron fist was now a setting in which the embryonic Manic Street Preachers first found their feet. The single was limited to only 300 copies of 7" vinyl, most of which were distributed to labels and magazines. Steven

Wells, the veteran music journalist, spotted the band's potential early and made Suicide Alley *NME*'s single of the week — a year after its initial release.

"Revolution soon dies sold out for a pay rise." New Art Riot EP sleeve

The band's next release in June 1990 was the *New Art Riot* EP, another wild-eyed introduction to the band's brand of chaotic punk rock. The EP was issued as a limited edition 12" vinyl of 1,000 copies by the independent label Damaged Goods. The lead track New Art Riot featured a strained shouted vocal from James Dean Bradfield over a scratchy stop-start riff that never really allowed the song to fully explode. The EP's standout track, Strip It Down, was a wonderful rush of Skids style punk that sounded like it had arrived via a rift in space and time direct from 1977. Strip It Down also had the honour of accompanying the band's first foray into music video performance. The promo featured the band miming the track within an ever-changing fractal tunnel of psychedelic patterns. The EP scored the lucrative 'Single of the Week' spot in *Melody Maker*. Richey Edwards was also now a fully-fledged member of the band, taking on the role of lyricist and rhythm guitarist. Though it was no secret he could barely string together a set of simple punk rock chords, his posturing on-stage made his guitar look like a lethal weapon. The EP's cover artwork was of a ragged European Union flag flapping in the wind, starting a trend in Manic Street Preachers records and singles to feature flags on the sleeve art.

On a gentleman's agreement, the Manic Street Preachers 'signed' a contract with the indie label Heavenly Records, home to dream-pop darlings Saint Etienne and Flowered Up. Heavenly would put out a few singles and have the band play gigs alongside other label acts until the band scored a better deal. It was the whirlwind rush of Motown Junk, released in January 1991 that broke the mould and brought the band to the attention of music critics and music fans that were still punk rock inclined.

Motown Junk was a gloriously nihilistic and iconoclastic declaration on the meaninglessness of modern culture, which unceremoniously (yet quite hilariously) insulted the legacy of John Lennon by insisting that the authors 'laughed' when Lennon was shot dead by Mark Chapman. Years later Bradfield admitted that the remarks were somewhat hasty: 'It was kind of a really blunt, uncivilised and undiplomatic,' but explained that 'Motown Junk was probably the first song where we actually could be the band we were inside our heads'.[5]

Motown Junk began with a sample of Public Enemy touting 'revolution revolution' continuously until Bradfield's distinctive riff breaks in and rattles away for the remainder of the song. The single's distinctive sleeve art of a wristwatch melted and twisted at the exact moment the Hiroshima bomb detonated was a visual indicator of the sonic mayhem contained within.

The next — and last — Heavenly release already indicated the band were straining against the indie label set-up. Released on May 7, 1991, You Love Us was a brilliantly sarcastic statement from a band that had had plenty of media exposure, but very little of it positive. The track began with a sample of Krzysztof Penderecki's haunting Threnody To The Victims Of Hiroshima, and finished with a coda that included the distinctive drum break of Iggy Pop's Lust For Life, a savage combination of high and low culture. Whilst Motown Junk was an explosive punk record, You Love Us was a more straight-ahead glam rock song desperate to burst out of its low-fi production values. James Dean Bradfield recalled in an interview with Simon Price that:

"Songs of love echo underclass betrayal." Motown Junk single sleeve

> Whereas on 'Motown Junk' our ambition is just to explode. On 'You Love Us' we're already failing to articulate what's in our heads. I remember Jeff (Barrett, head of Heavenly) saying 'Um, it kind of reminds me of Thin Lizzy'. And we were thinking 'Yeah, so?! What's wrong with that? Thin Lizzy with our lyrics! Cool!'[6]

You could take the boys out of the Valleys...

For the band's debut record, *Generation Terrorists*, You Love Us was re-recorded with a more hard rock production value that did indeed become a kind of Thin Lizzy tribute. The samples were dropped and instead of the Lust For Life coda a wicked Bradfield guitar solo led the track to its conclusion.

Manic Street Preachers made the leap from indie to major label, signing with Sony UK imprint, Columbia Records. Released in February 1992, the band's major label debut *Generation Terrorists,* was a sprawling mosaic of punk rock and heavy metal that defined the band's agenda, determination, and audacity. The band felt convinced the record would sell in its millions, and thus with their legacy soon to be set in stone, it would be the first and last record they would ever need to record. This was not the case.

This impudence in the face of such conflicting music scenes and styles certainly brought the notice of the music press. However, the contrast in style and sound also made them look somewhat cartoonish, outdated, and in comparison to the earnest Seattleites, and hedonistic scallies of Manchester, not to be taken seriously as the signifiers of a new musical movement. The press certainly didn't think so. Coverage of the band often began and ended with xenophobic references to their Welsh heritage.

This lack of respect was the cause for one of the band's most dramatic early moments. A confrontation between Edwards and *NME* journalist Steve Lamacq (later to host BBC Radio 1's *Evening Sessions*) on the subject of integrity led Edwards to reach for a razor blade and carve '4 REAL' into his forearm. The shocking images were front page news in the music press and gave the band plenty of media attention. The whole episode was strung together for a short audio documentary Sleeping With The NME, included in the band's 1992 standalone single Theme From M∗A∗S∗H (Suicide Is Painless).

However, few rock bands at this time had the guile to achieve so much and then throw it away at the apparent height of their game. Manic Street Preachers had that intention and they would achieve it by willingly prostituting themselves to any outlet willing to give them the time. They played the game so well at the beginning of their career that they easily courted the indie music press (*NME*), the hard rock press (*Kerrang!*), and even mainstream teeny magazines (*Smash Hits!*). They had the opportunity to warp the minds of Britain's preteens by performing the proto-metal single Love's Sweet

Exile on kids' TV show *Motormouth*. A year later the band would appear on another British kids' show *Gimmie 5* performing From Despair To Where which featured the surreal scene of the show's puppet host, Nobby the Sheep, moshing to a song that dealt with the traumas of everyday life.

"Culture sucks down words."
Generation Terrorists single sleeve

*Generation Terrorists* veered from politicized subjects such as the evils of capitalism and third world economics (Slash N' Burn), denouncing the British monarchy (Repeat UK), the loss of individualism in a modern capitalist society (Love's Sweet Exile), prostitution (Little Baby Nothing), the banking system (NatWest, Barclays, Midlands, Lloyds) and the burden of being a budding rock star (Condemned To Rock And Roll). The subject of being a Manic Street Preacher would also crop up numerous times during the record, especially on Stay Beautiful, and You Love Us, a theme that would continue across their career. Lyrically, the record was astounding in its intelligence and complexity. The listening experience could be likened to taking courses in economics, political science, cultural studies, philosophy, with a night school class in rock history all in the same instant. Forget Slavoj Žižek, Manic Street Preachers were the first rock star Marxist philosophers to engage with an audience. If indeed *Generation Terrorists* had been the band's one and only statement, the listener would have established everything they needed to know about the political outlook from the eighteen tracks included.

Despite it being designed for mass consumption, *Generation Terrorists* was not always a winning formula for international success, as James Dean Bradfield reflected twenty years later in an interview with *Q Magazine*: 'I don't know about glorious but it was a monumental failure [*laughs*]. We'd announced our own greatness without having much to back it up.'[7] The contradictory fusion of punk ethics and stadium rock was not what the masses were crying out for. Songs such as the now-prophetic (in the wake of the 2008 financial crash) NatWest, Barclays, Midlands, Lloyds, with its theme of capitalist corruption via four very British banks, held no appeal to an audience outside of the UK. A lazy reworking of Repeat by Public Enemy's producers, The Bomb Squad, could not translate the anti-royal sentiment of the original song. The record's fourth track, Motorcycle Emptiness, with its mournful guitar solo and rousing chorus was a bona fide mainstream song, but the sombre lyrics ('life lies a slow suicide' and 'itemise loathing and feed yourself smiles') would wash over the heads of most hard rock fans nurtured on hair metal bands like Skid Row and Mötley Crüe, who mostly sang about drugs, fast cars, and bikini-clad girls girls girls. The song was not given a live outing till much later in the band's touring schedule due to the shabby venues they were still playing and the cheap equipment they used. The grandeur of Motorcycle Emptiness was not designed for small, sweaty club venues but for wide open spaces provided by stadia that were, at this point at least, eluding them.

What is remarkable about *Generation Terrorists* is the album's absolute unwillingness to sound like anything else in British music at the time. With the emergence of the Madchester music scene, influenced in some respects by Northern Soul and Chicago house music and signified by bands like The Happy Mondays, Primal Scream and The Stone Roses, Manic Street Preachers did not follow suit. Nor did they resemble piss-weak, jangly indie bands like The Wonderstuff or Teenage Fanclub, though some of their early Blackwood demos did incorporate that fey element, especially the wonderfully cutesy Behave Yourself Baby and Go Buzz Baby Go, both of which included parts that would be pillaged and incorporated into Motorcycle Emptiness. The record wears its influence on its sleeves, and those influences were often deeply unpopular at the time. Punk rock was long dead, glam rock was in the gutter, and intelligence in lyricism was over since the end of The Smiths. In 1992 *Generation Terrorists* stuck out like a sore thumb. But it's also credit to the band that they persisted and remained resilient. This attribution would continue throughout their career.

The band's use of quotations from philosophers, authors and sportsmen on their record sleeves started with *Generation Terrorists* and continued throughout. Inside *Generation Terrorists*' bright pink and blue inlay — a cover image that featured Richey Edwards' torso with his 'Useless Generation' tattoo modified into the album's title — quotes from the likes of Sylvia Plath, EE Cummings and Valerie Solanas explained the meaning behind each song. *Generation Terrorists* was a bold statement of intent, a complete package of audio and literary stimuli.

Though it sold in respectful numbers for a debut record, the sense of defeatism by *Generation Terrorists*' underperformance soon prevailed for the band that had placed so much emphasis on its success. The band's aesthetic and sound needed a more palatable direction and so with *Gold Against the Soul* they honed their more straight-edge American influences and courted the hard rock magazine like *Kerrang!* and *Raw.*

The kindling of this more mature hard rock sound could be found in the charity single Theme From M*A*S*H (Suicide Is Painless) a song that the band had released during the *Generation Terrorists* campaign in September 1992 as a double A-side with Irish art rockers The Fatima Mansions cover of Bryan Adams' syrupy love song (Everything I Do) I Do It For You. The original version of Suicide Is Painless, written by Johnny Mandel and Mike Altman (son of film director Robert Altman, and director of the *M*A*S*H* film) was a mournful oddity that nevertheless stirred the soul with its simplicity and poetic lyricism ('the sword of time will pierce our skin'). Manic Street Preachers' version cranked up the amps and concluded the song with a guitar driven rock out that was reminiscent of Guns N' Roses' hard rock cover of Wings' Live And Let Die. The song earned the band their first top ten single.

MANIC STREET PREACHERS' TONED-DOWN AND MATURE sounding second album, *Gold Against the Soul* (1993), featured a slender ten tracks of more-or-less straightforward rock, with lyrics that didn't require a degree in cultural studies and political theory to fully comprehend. In fact the lyrics dealt mostly with the personal as opposed to the political. It expanded upon the more emotional thoughts of Theme From M*A*S*H. The band's dash of vibrant pinks and blues witnessed on *Generation Terrorists* were subdued into dark brown sepia tones. In some respects, *Gold Against the Soul* did win over a more mainstream audience, as well as giving the band a supporting gig with Bon Jovi at the massive Milton Keynes Bowl. With *Generation Terrorists*, the Manic Street Preachers had earned themselves a devoted fan base on their own terms, but the desire to conquer *all* music listeners the

"Radio nostalgia is radio death." Gold Against The Soul sleeve

world over had obviously eluded them. *Gold Against the Soul* contained straight-ahead radio friendly rock pop that tailored the Manic Street Preachers' ear for a rousing chorus to a mature, stadium-filled setting. The record's lyrical concerns were more personal and reflective compared with *Generation Terrorists* political and cultural analysis. The Manic Street Preachers had grown up (well in fact they were still only in their early twenties) and soldiered on and the verve and vigour that came with their youthful pronouncements of world domination were now a naïve memory.

The crisp soft rock and mature attire of *Gold Against the Soul* did not satisfy the Manic Street Preachers' sense of theatrics. The band returned in August 1994 in rude form with *The Holy Bible*, one of the bravest and most musically accomplished records of the decade. With its deeply disturbing imagery,

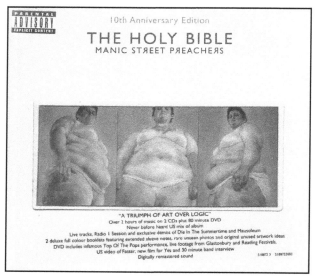

"Be pure — be vigilant — behave."
*The Holy Bible* tenth anniversary album sleeve

both lyrical and in its physical artwork (the record came in a shocking Jenny Saville sleeve and was adorned in quotes from *The Torture Garden*), *The Holy Bible* was a testament to the dark pre-millennial tension that was building up as the century began its closing chapter. Returning to their more urgent punk origins, Manic Street Preachers also drew on their desire to match music with stylistics, dressing themselves in mismatched secondhand military attire with spray painted slogans ('I'm so modern that everything is pointless') and Goth makeup. This was a deliberate attempt to regain control of their music and aesthetics that had set them apart from the emerging Britpop scene, much like they had set themselves apart from the dominant Baggy and Shoegaze scene a few years earlier.

Whilst *Gold Against the Soul* had been made in the plush Hookend Manor studio with all kinds of distractions and vices at hand, *The Holy Bible* was recorded in Sound Space, a tiny cheap demo studio in a red-light district of Cardiff. The band also gave themselves a regimented schedule, recording the album in day shifts. James Dean Bradfield called it 'method recording', and 'wanted that kind of utilitarian vibe to try and rub off in the music.'[8] The approach worked in spectacular form.

*The Holy Bible* was a success in ridding themselves of the corporate rock stigma, but in terms of sales it reduced their fan base to only the most devoted core. Any causal rock listener the band had picked up with the commercial sounds of *Gold Against the Soul* was instantly turned away by *The Holy Bible*'s abrasive structure. The music, regimented and grinding as it was, offered moments of bliss and heady riffs, but the lyrical concerns of anorexia (4st 7lbs), the Holocaust (Intense Humming Of Evil), and a pro-capital punishment song (Archives Of Pain) meant the songs couldn't cross the mainstream threshold. Plus the forth word on the record was 'cunt', and they'd be plenty more of that.

However, this loss in commercial appreciation was replaced by a critical lauding that had previously never been forthcoming from the music press. Most critics agreed that *The Holy Bible* was a devastatingly brilliant record of lyrical intelligence and musical accomplishment. *The Holy Bible* shared a similar artistic vision to Nirvana's difficult, and lyrically disturbing third album, *In Utero* (1993*)*, a record that also sought to shed a casual fanbase of rock jocks after the band's success with *Nevermind* (1991). *The Holy Bible* remains the Manics' most appreciated album by fans and critics alike. However, behind the scenes the band was disintegrating. Richey Edwards was struggling to cope with his many conditions that included alcoholism, anorexia, depression, and self-harm. His absence from most of the band's summer festival appearances triggered rumours of nervous breakdowns and suicide attempts. A tour of Thailand in the spring of 1994 was chronicled by the *NME*, and by all accounts it was a bizarre and bewildering experience, which saw Edwards entering into a dangerous frame of mind and self-harm. As Edwards took a leave of absence over the summer, the remaining band members continued to perform, marching to the beat of their traditional working class ethos. Edwards spent a number of months prior to the release of *The Holy Bible* in the Priory, a clinic popular with musicians, models, actors and celebrities. The clinic's twelve-step programme relied heavily on religious symbolism to create order in one's life. The Priory's effects on Edwards were short-lived, his intelligence deciphered the programme, and band members were even suspect of the programme, with Nicky Wire stating to the *NME* that Edwards 'quickly realised, when he was in The Priory... that the cure basically means having to destroy the entire entity that you are.'[9]

In January 1995, Richey Edwards disappeared and was never seen or heard from again. The media attention around the disappearance placed the remaining Manic Street Preachers under greater scrutiny and their next step would be intensely monitored.

The band's return was actually low-key, at least initially. A cover of Hal David and Burt Bacharach's Raindrops Keep Falling On My Head appeared on the 1995 War Child charity record, *The Help Album*. The song was far subtler and more spacious than any of the band's previous output, and even featured a haunting, yet strangely uplifting trumpet solo from Sean Moore. The lyrics were sullen, yet also hopeful of resolution. It linked to the forthcoming *Everything Must Go*, yet also aligned the band with Britpop and its forefathers. Other recordings on *The Help Album* featured Paul Weller and Paul McCartney covering The Beatles' Come Together as The Smokin' Mojo Filters, old touring mates Suede, bitter enemies The Levellers, plus Radiohead, The Boo Radleys, and of course Britpop superstars, Oasis. Though it was for a righteous cause, the band's decision to hide within the track listing of other bands and artists could be considered a wise move. Not yet ready to carry the full burden of facing up to their past, it allowed the subject of Edwards' disappearance to be diffused and meant the band could move forward with a new approach.

Fourteen months after the disappearance of Richey Edwards, the Manic Street Preachers reassessed their provocative stance and came back with the gloriously sweeping single A Design For Life, a song that distilled the working class psyche in sparse yet evocative couplets matched with a widescreen musical accompaniment. The band's image, record design and live performances were intentionally blank and nondescript, allowing none to read any significance into their actions, or to draw unwanted sympathy from fans and critics. At this point, the band very much wanted to signal the music with little acknowledgement of their troubled past. Design For Life all at once sounded like a jump for joy and sigh of relief.

Although beautifully produced and hugely successful, the album *Everything Must Go* (1996) for once gave the band a platform in which to prod and provoke its listeners, and talk openly about their socialist leanings, their diverse influences in music and literature. It was a platform they chose not to put to good use, especially in the absence of the band's main provocateur. The Manic Street Preachers instead played it

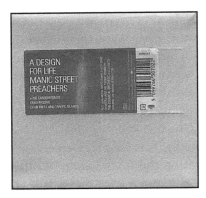

A DESIGN
FOR LIFE
MANIC STREET
PREACHERS

"Libraries gave us power."
Design For Life single sleeve

fairly safe, and whilst two years earlier they appeared on *Top of the Pops* dressed in terrorist-style balaclavas ploughing through a raucous version of *The Holy Bible's* first single Faster, they now appeared regularly on irreverent TV shows like *TFI Friday*, or *The White Room* dressed in corduroy jackets and combat trousers, and being matey with Noel and Liam Gallagher of Oasis. Their new respectable style also made them palatable for the middle class/middle aged audiences of *Later... With Jools Holland*, on which they appeared on numerous times. The lyrics on *Everything Must Go*, although rich with emotion and circumstance, were perhaps the least political the band had ever written, although, in the era of laddish Britpop, the band's natural intelligence shone through the more mundane and dumb aspects of that brief musical excursion.

THE DIFFERENCES WITH PRE- AND POST- RICHEY MANIC Street Preachers was so enormous that it was hard to believe it was the same band performing. In effect, it no longer was. *Everything Must Go* marked the beginning of the 'post-Richey' era that would go on to define the Manic Street Preachers in the national consciousness. This was Manics MK II. Although the album contained songs penned by Edwards they were far away from the harrowing and urgent postpunk of *The Holy*

*Bible*. The beautiful and elegant Small Black Flowers That Grow In The Sky was simple acoustic guitar, plucked harp, and James Dean Bradfield's yearning voice, only its lyrical imagery of caged animals gave away the song's true darkness.

Musical accompaniment to the Edwards penned The Girl Who Wanted To Be God' was by far the most

"Escape from our history."
Everything Must Go single sleeve

unexpected. The track's lush orchestration and glorious chorus was the flipside of *The Holy Bible*'s harrowing compositions. The Nirvana-like Removables was the only song that would have sat comfortably with *The Holy Bible*'s harsher sounds. Its rambling lyric of 'aimless rut of my own perception' and dour acoustic musical accompaniment captured perfectly the author's utter despair. The song's inclusion on *Everything Must Go* would have no doubt made some of the new Manic Street Preachers fans jump for the skip button. The rest of the album was packed full of lush, string-drenched rock songs that dispensed with the outright political topics and personal self-loathing of previous records. In fact, songs such as Everything Must Go and the euphoric Australia spoke of escaping their own history and starting afresh.

The lyrics of Nicky Wire, which up until this point had been buried under Edwards' political/personal conflicts, had a more universal and less intrusive appeal. The crisp orchestration and euphoria of *Everything Must Go* was a reaction to *The Holy Bible*'s scathing worldview. A mood of cautious optimism prevailed in tracks such as Australia and the gorgeous Interiors (Song For Willim De Kooning). Yet the most blatant optimism was found on the track Further Away, the band's first unashamed love song. Manic Street Preachers had done something unprecedented. They had broken from their troubled past and forged a new identity for themselves. The lyrical brilliance, aesthetic beauty, and undeniable coolness of Edwards would linger with them forever, even as they became one of the most successful British bands of the decade and beyond.

During this period it was hard not to cast the Manic Street Preachers onto the Britpop pile. They adorned the covers of *Select*, *NME* and *Melody Maker*, alongside Oasis, Blur and Pulp. Their comeback song, Design For Life, with its chorus holler of 'we only wanna get drunk' had been somewhat misinterpreted as a drinking anthem and gave pissed-up Kangol wearing lads in provincial towns an excuse to throw their arms around each other and shout the song's chorus into the night sky. It stands shoulder to shoulder with Oasis' brittle Wonderwall, Blur's cheeky Girls And Boys, the class call to arms of Pulp's Common People, Ocean Colour Scene's steady Riverboat Song and Supergrass' chirpy hit Alright as a bona fide Britpop anthem. These songs define the carefree lark and pissed-up misadventures of the mid 1990s. How do I know this? Because I was one of those pissed-up provincial boys who sang them on his way merrily home after kicking out time from the local boozer.

Although they stood miles apart from the petty squabbling of Oasis and Blur and the phony posturing of chancers like Menswear or Sleeper, their mainstream acceptance by the music industry press meant that they lazily got lumped in with the trendy mob of Britpop stalwarts. In the year that

*Everything Must Go* was released the Manic Street Preachers went from featuring predominantly in the *NME* and *Kerrang!* to being the cover stars in the more upscale music mags, *Q Magazine* and *Mojo* on a regular basis. Their triumphant double whammy win for Best Band and Best Album at the 1997 Brit Awards sealed their national popularity, even as Wire used his acceptance speech to promote the importance of UK comprehensive schools. The band even did the unthinkable and embraced other popular bands and artists with collaborations. James Dean Bradfield united with Australian songstress Kylie Minogue on her 1997 'indie' album *Impossible Princess*, co-writing the songs Some Kind Of Bliss and I Don't Need Anyone. Nicky Wire teamed up with Lightning Seeds frontman Ian Brodie on the song Waiting For Today To Happen. Bradfield also added vocals to the dreamy electronica of 808 State's single Lopez.

The Manic Street Preachers triumph over tragedy was in a way a metaphor for the late nineties itself. The proposed era of Cool Britannia and Britpop had allowed rock stars to wine and dine with prime ministers in the corridors of power. The dark recession of the early to late-eighties and early nineties had given way to a newfound optimism that came with the New Labour government. Under the leadership of Tony Blair and his free market loving chancellor, Gordon Brown, New Labour had become the political wing of the Britpop movement. The Manic Street Preachers were never ones to engage the mainstream British media, preferring to remain in the music press and broadsheets rather than the tabloids and gossip rags. So whilst the bands of Britpop and the notion of Cool Britannia disintegrated around them, the Manic Street Preachers battened down the hatches and waited out the storm.

By the time of their return in 1998 with the single If You

Tolerate This Your Children Will Be Next the musical landscape had changed dramatically. The British guitar bands that had latched onto the coattails of Britpop were all but gone, burnt out on drugs, booze, and ego. The bands that had defined the lark and lavishness of the era had moved on in sound and style. Blur had ditched the cheeky-chappie façade that had defined them on *Parklife* (1994) and *The Great Escape* (1995) and embraced an American lo-fi experimental aesthetic with their self-titled 1997 record. Radiohead, the band that was always destined for stadia with thoughtful paeans such as High And Dry and Fake Plastic Trees, had recorded *OK Computer* (1997), an album bursting with experimentation, existential angst, and pre-millennium tension, which would come to fruition with their next album, the post-millennial and mostly electronic *Kid A* (2000). Pulp had followed up their mega-selling 1996 album, *Different Class*, with *This is Hardcore* (1998), an album of throbbing sexual torch songs. Oasis, the most renowned band of the Britpop excess, had not been so lucky. Although still hugely successful as a live act, Oasis were on a downward trajectory which had started with the band's bloated and uninspired third record *Be Here Now* (1997) and continued into the utter irrelevance of *Standing on the Shoulder of Giants* (2000). The early everyman anthems that Noel Gallagher had crafted whilst working on a building site had given away to stale odes to his band's success, his own greatness and desire for drugs and materialism with guest musicians such as Johnny Depp joining in.

Manic Street Preachers' next record, *This is My Truth Tell Me Yours*, released September 1998, was an album about regaining identity and was the band's most openly Welsh record. The subject of the songs varied, but one common theme remained: a sense of personal defeat. This was perhaps most clear on the record's very first track, the sombre The Everlasting, that recalls the optimistic era of the band's early years when 'we were winning' in comparison to their current physical and mental condition. *This is My Truth...* was an album that talked of the sadness of achieving success without Richey Edwards in tow and without their youthful

"My ideology it is dead and gone." This Is My Truth Tell Me Yours single sleeve

vigour intact. Though all the members of the band were only in their late twenties at the time of recording, it sounded like they'd lived a lifetime of hurt. The album's third track and also third single, You Stole The Sun From My Heart, might have had a raucous bouncy chorus that got people bopping at the indie disco, but the lyrics were completely sour, the author reflecting that he had to 'stop smiling' and public displays of happiness as it gave 'the wrong impression' about his true internal feelings. The record's fifth track, Tsunami, also contained a euphoric chorus, yet the lyrical concern was June and Jennifer Gibbons, identical twins who grew up in Wales and gave up talking when they were children, committed a number of petty crimes and ended up locked up in Broadmoor Hospital with the likes of serial killer Peter Sutcliffe. The line 'Disco dancing with the rapists' summed up the absurdity of the Gibbon sisters' situation, but it was also a line that, as the song burst out of the speakers at any indie disco, could be chanted with glee at the lecherous blokes populating the dance floor.

*This is My Truth...* was also the first record to be solely authored by Nicky Wire, and it showed. The lyrics were mostly domestic in origin. The furthest the record ventured was to the Spanish battlefields of the civil war in If You Tolerate This Your Children Will Be Next, and even this was seen through the eyes of the Welsh farmers who joined the International Brigade to fight against fascism. Wire had found a more profound and personal voice that was revelatory. Born A Girl lingered on the premise of Wire's desire to shed his masculinity completely and not be 'this mess of a man'. Despite Bradfield's very male persona voicing the song, its tenderness was delicate and absolute. Whilst Black Dog On My Shoulder was an ode to a depression that continually poked and prodded at Wire's psyche.

Musically, *This is My Truth...* lacked the euphoria of *Everything Must Go*. The dazzling choruses of Tsunami and You Stole The Sun From My Heart were its only true anthems, but their subject matter was a betrayal. Nonetheless, with a solid number one single and expectations high for the Manic Street Preachers' next major release, *This is My Truth...* sold phenomenally well in the United Kingdom and saw the band gain a moderate platform throughout Europe, Asia, and Australia. The American market still eluded them. An album of sombre Welsh-centric songs wouldn't necessarily gel with a US audience currently sending the likes of Blink 182, Sum 41, Slipknot and Marilyn Manson up the rock charts. And certainly the political jurisdiction of *This is My Truth...* was predominantly that of the Welsh valleys. From the record's title, a quotation taken from Welsh Labour politician and founder of the National Health Service, Aneurin Bevan, to the album's fourth track Ready For Drowning, which mirrored the intentional flooding of the Welsh village of Capel Celyn to supply drinking water to Liverpool, with that of the Welsh tendency to drown one's sorrows in alcohol (and one could point out the much-discussed fate of Richey Edwards). When the album's political content did step further afield, it tended to disappoint, such as the studio experimentation of the song S.Y.M.M. (South Yorkshire Mass Murderer), a song that failed to deal with the subject of the Hillsborough disaster, the tragic event that occurred during a football match between Liverpool and Nottingham Forest in April 1989, in which ninety-six people were killed in a human crush. The inspiration for the song was not taken from firsthand experience, but from a Jimmy McGovern penned episode of the British TV series *Cracker,* hence the lyric 'thank you Jimmy McGovern for reminding me of what lives on'. The song's title was the most confrontational element and even garnered comments from then South Yorkshire's Assistant Chief Constable Ian Daines, who was as quoted in the *NME*: 'Judging solely from the title it would appear to be in bad taste and is likely to cause offence to many people.'[10] Though one might assume that if Assistant Chief Constable Daines had actually listened to the lyrical content of the track he might have not bothered to comment at all.

Whilst previous records had felt very traditional in sound, by means of utilising the obvious band dynamic of vocals, guitar, bass and drums, *This is My Truth...* had a synthetic quality that was captured quite obviously on S.Y.M.M. with its studio experimentation of backward drums and treated guitars. You Stole The Sun From My Heart featured a drum loop sampled from a pinball machine, If You Tolerate This... utilised effects pedals and recalibrated traditional sounds using Pro Tools software to create a futuristic quality. This futurism would be explored in the single's promotional video. It featured the band trapped in a brightly lit room and wired up to an unseen machine, forced to play the song until they are physically sick. A faceless family frolic within the same compound.

Building on the success of *Everything Must Go*, the Manic Street Preachers again won Best Band and Best Album at the 1999 BRIT Awards, sealing their status as one of Britain's biggest bands. This time they accepted the award, after a functionary performance of You Stole The Sun..., by Bradfield bellowing out the band's name into the microphone, whilst Wire whipped out a skipping rope and jumped a few lines. Whereas in 1997 the award had felt deserved and the status of underdog was still levelled at them, the 1999 win felt like the industry swinging awards in the direction of guaranteed big record sales. Nicky Wire in an interview with *Q Magazine* two years later reflected that 'the first time it felt like we were outsiders coming in. The second time it just felt we were insiders and we were already part of the establishment. It was a pretty hollow night'.[11]

Despite aligning themselves with the music establishment (though still standing apart), Manic Street Preachers had achieved something profound. The band had emerged victorious to be embraced by a much larger and more mainstream audience. They had traversed the dicey musical escapades of Manchester Baggy, Shoegaze, Hair Metal, Grunge, and Britpop and charted a new path for themselves. But changes were afoot. At the press conference to announce their New Year's Eve concert at Cardiff's Millennium Stadium, James Dean Bradfield hinted that they would be focusing on their next record: 'We want to concentrate on making the best album we can possibly make.'[12] It was a bold statement for a record that would need to redefine the band in the new century.

# KNOWING *KNOW YOUR ENEMY*

IN THE AFTERMATH OF *THIS IS MY TRUTH...* IT WAS HARD to make a case for Manic Street Preachers being an outsider rock band, or a truly socialist one for that matter. Whilst they absolutely remained from the working class, their major success had placed a huge distance between the band they once were — snotty eyeliner clad punk provocateurs with a Camus quote — and the one they had become — award-winning establishment players. But, of course this was a destination they had always promised to arrive at. Though they had never been political activists, preferring to raise awareness of events and situations via song lyrics, a lyrical current had always run through them that gestured towards them being anti-establishment and anti-capitalist. The first sign they were in trouble was during the band's 1999 Glastonbury Festival appearance. Not only was the headlining performance a by-the-numbers run through of hits past and present, but it was a lumbering slog of a set that failed to produce much energy or enthusiasm from the band or audience.

Five years earlier, during their midday set at the same festival in 1994, Nicky Wire had stood at the microphone and proclaimed how much he'd like to see a few bypasses built over the 'shithole' that was Glastonbury. Wire was perhaps debating a modernist solution to traffic congestion, but now it seemed the band was playing nice. Wire barely made a peep from his microphone all night. The situation was made worse by the band bringing with them their very own portable lavatory, exclusively for their use whilst at Glastonbury. Staunch socialist Billy Bragg made the revelation in the *NME*, posting a picture with a crudely scrawled note stuck to the door that read: 'These facilities are reserved exclusively for the Manic Street Preachers.'[13] It was a somewhat humiliating event that was referred to in the music press as 'crappergate'. Manic Street Preachers' egalitarian principles had been shattered. They wouldn't allow the great unwashed, in this case other bands who were performing at the festival, to share their facilities. Bragg even called out the band's political stance:

> Maybe that was the thing that bugged me — that the Manics were doing this against the spirit of Glastonbury. That it was contrary to the band's professed ideals didn't surprise me as it seems like it has been a while since they thought about what their politics are now.
>
> If Nicky Wire has anything to say about that aspect of their current behaviour, rather than just shooting his mouth off about how hurt his pride is, then I would be happy to have a discussion with him about walking it like you talk it.[14]

Of course Wire didn't take Bragg up on his offer. One couldn't help but think that if the band had brought the portable toilet with them to the 1992 Reading Festival it would have been a brilliant punk rock gesture, but in 1999 with millions of record sales in the bag, it left a bad smell.

In retrospect this event signalled a change in the band's stance. For too long it had seemed like Manic Street Preachers had played the courteous band. The music establishment had finally embraced them and showered them with awards and praise, but this had come at a price. When the band made their live return a few months after Glastonbury in August 1999 at the V Festival the fire in their belly had been rekindled. Before they launched into a blazing rendition of Tsunami, Wire took to the stand and stated: 'This is for Billy Bragg, I wouldn't let him piss in my toilet for all the money in the world. Get back to the army, you dickhead, and stop stealing Woody Guthrie's songs.'[15] Although his remarks were juvenile, it was remarkable to once again hear Wire run his motormouth off and launch an attack on an established left-leaning artist such as Bragg. In their early days they had often slammed Slowdive as awful indie drivel, called The Levellers a bunch of crusties, Morrissey a has-been, and aimed a death wish at R.E.M.'s singer Michael Stipe, but too much mingling at the Brit Awards and with other bands of their ilk had softened them. As the band trashed their instruments (always a sign of a band's deliverance) Wire lifted his tiny leopard print dress and revealed a pair of skimpy briefs to the audience. Change was afoot.

As the century came to its close the release of the one-off single, Masses Against The Classes, was a hint at what was to come. Though at the time no one could have truly known what was around the corner, not even the band itself. Masses Against The Classes was an urgent and nostalgic two fingered salute to the end of the century. It wasn't to be taken seriously as a potential new direction for the band. Masses marked the band's second number one single in the UK charts and had the prestige of being the first UK number one single of the twenty-first century. The single was deleted on day of release, leaving whatever copies remained in stores to be snapped up

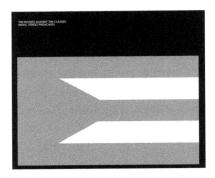

"Hello it's us again." Masses Against
The Classes single sleeve

by the band's devotees. The song title itself came from a William Gladstone quotation and was bookended with a sample from American political commentator Noam Chomsky ('The country was founded on the principle that the primary role of government is to protect property from the majority, and so it remains.') and Bradfield's howl of French philosopher Albert Camus ('The slave begins by demanding justice and ends by wanting to wear a crown.') that harked back to the sample-heavy days of Motown Junk. Yet, the single's sleeve acted as a premonition to *Know Your Enemy*. The cover artwork came adorned with a Cuban flag (curiously without its socialist star) against a plain black background. At the time it felt meaningless. The Cuban flag and CCP communist chic was everywhere. High street clothing retailers were selling hooded tops, jackets and t-shirts emblazoned with the Cuban flag, and hammer and sickle. The iconography of Che Guevara was plastered all over the walls of student digs the world over. In the case of Manic Street Preachers, all this could be considered a sign that a shift was happening in the political consciousness of the band.

Despite the triumphalism of the last few years, gaining a popular audience with *Everything Must Go* and *This is My Truth...* seemed to place the band into a reactionary mindset upon their return in April 2001 with *Know Your Enemy*. The title alone took a defiant tone. This defiance was directed towards themselves with Nicky Wire admitting in an interview with *Q Magazine* that the enemy of *Enemy* was 'what we had become.'[16] To quote from Sun Tzu's *The Art of War*, a key text in strategy and war:

> If you know the enemy and know yourself, you need not fear the result of a hundred battles. If you know yourself but not the enemy, for every victory gained you will also suffer a defeat. If you know neither the enemy nor yourself, you will succumb in every battle.[17]

In this case, the band wanted to rediscover a part of their past and to *know* it once again and learn from it, but also to realise that without an enemy, either external or internal the band's purpose was absent.

The spilling-out-the-pub anthems were mostly gone from *Know Your Enemy*. No Design For Life, no Australia, no You Stole The Sun From My Heart. In its place, sixteen tracks of abrasive punk rock dirges, breezy west coast rock and a disco song. *Know Your Enemy* took some unpacking. The record's flip-flopping approach to the normalities of album track listing was destabilizing to say the least. One moment a straight-up Manic Street Preachers mosher (Intravenous Agnostic) that would get the indie kids jumping, the next a bluesy Wire-led dirge (Wattsville Blues). *Know Your Enemy* was as antagonistic and full of bile as *The Holy Bible*, in fact more so, and the reach this time round was far wider. Songs such as Royal Correspondent were spiteful, whilst Wattsville Blues seemed particularly potent with utter resentment towards 'every single living organism'.

The record caused much confusion among fans and critics who had highly praised the band from the *Everything Must Go* era onwards. Review data from Metacritic.com gives the record a metascore of fifty-seven making it the lowest on the list, yet its user score rates it second from top, just under *Journal for Plague Lovers* (worth baring in mind that Metacritic began in 1999 and only aggregates reviews from this point onwards).

James Dean Bradfield, in an interview with *Incendiary Magazine*, stated that the record alienated 'at least a million people who had bought our previous two albums.'[18] It was interesting to think that the band now had a million fans they could potentially alienate without too much loss. Those that had been with the band from Motown Junk onwards might have welcomed the antagonistic front the band had laid on. In the press Nicky Wire had regained a passion for snotty quips and verbal attacks on other bands, and stated in an interview with *Q Magazine* that *Know Your Enemy* was the record they should have made 'when we first came out',[19] an interesting statement to make considering *Generation Terrorists* divided so much opinion at the time and ultimately failed to set the world alight commercially. Wire even went on to suggest that *Know Your Enemy* was 'one of the best albums of all time'[20]

However, commercial returns seemed to be the last thing on the band's mind. Even *Know Your Enemy*'s album sleeve was in contrast to previous Manic Street Preachers' records. The crisp, clean, minimalist sleeve designs from *Gold Against the Soul* onwards were replaced with a colourful, vibrant and noisy cover by Welsh urban artist Neale Howells. Howells' sleeve art was certainly reflective of the album's mash-up of genres and the newfound urgency. The sleeve resembled a blood-soaked wall after a revolution had overthrown a corrupt regime. As well as designing the *Know Your Enemy* album sleeve, Howells' work also appeared on the sleeves for the record's subsequent single releases.

Although *Know Your Enemy* was a somewhat bloated

sixteen tracks, their longest long player since *Generation Terrorists*, there is a genuine case for proclaiming the band brave at the very least for unleashing such a momentous beast on an unsuspecting public. The band dismissed the polish of *Everything Must Go*, and *This is My Truth...* instead recording an album of diverse styles and confrontational lyrics, which cultivated a raw production value that harked back to the singles and EPs of the Damaged Goods and Heavenly Records era, but also referenced the postpunk of *The Holy Bible*. *Know Your Enemy* was a an attempt to shed some of the newer casual fans who had latched on in recent years, yet in many ways it was also a record designed to delight the older fans that had long given up hope of Manic Street Preachers releasing something akin to *Know Your Enemy*.

Despite this, *Know Your Enemy* is perhaps one of the least liked records by fans (depending on the fan, possibly lingering behind *Lifeblood*, or *Postcards From a Young Man*) and critics (though the record at the time usually scored about 7.5 with critics at the time). Ultimately the record is a reactionary piece of work to what the band had 'done in the past', as Nicky Wire commented to Simon Price in the *Guardian*: 'When you reach contentment in life, it's difficult to express anything. It had just got boring.'[21] *Know Your Enemy* is the band's solid reaction to boredom.

The record stood no chance of being sold in America due to its launch taking place at the Karl Marx Theatre in Havana, Cuba (more of which later), and the continuing embargo that was put in place by America on the Cuban government in 1960 after Fidel Castro and his 'Barbudos' (bearded ones) overthrew the government of the 'friendly dictator' Fulgencio Batista. The irony of this was that *Know Your Enemy* was by far the most American sounding record the Manic Street Preachers had recorded since *Generation Terrorists'* Guns N' Roses/New York Dolls sonic tribute. From the Queens of the Stone Age-like opener Found That Soul, to the harmonious Beach Boys sounding So Why So Sad and Year Of Purification, to the lo-fi distortions reminiscent of Sonic Youth in My Guernica and The Convalescent. Bizarrely, the album's American music homage is attached to a curious anti-American/consumerist lyricism (Let Robeson Sing, Baby Elian, Freedom Of Speech Won't Feed My Children), whose seeds can be traced all the way back to *Generation Terrorists* on songs like Tennessee ('your dreams can never earn enough') and Dead Yankee Drawl, a B-side to Little Baby Nothing, which mocked the hare-brained films *Bill and Ted* and *Wayne's World* and denounced American cultural and political dominance as 'turning one dollar into another and another', and of course the charging Ifwhiteamericatoldthetruthforonedayit'sworldwouldfallapart from *The Holy Bible*, which instructed the listener to 'fuck the Brady Bill' and that American 'morals only run as deep as the surface'.

In order to understand *Know Your Enemy*'s diversity and difference from Manic Street Preachers past releases let us now delve into the record itself. What follows is a track by track deconstruction of the record that allows us to see why in some respects the record was so perplexing, yet also how it matches with past records and acts as a pointer towards future recordings.

Found That Soul acts as a perfect gateway into *Know Your Enemy*'s punkier aspects, but it also acts as a mission statement of the Manic Street Preachers' mindset and intentions for the record itself. The song is a direct comment on the last few years of immense popularity and acts as a reclaiming of their past and future as a musical/political entity. The opening guitar riff is quickly joined by a ramshackle organ and drum motif that creates a fresh sonic blast. Bradfield's vocal is growly and deep and oddly sinister on the verses, yet the chorus is joyous in its simplicity. Musically the track is reminiscent of past B-side Prologue To History, another track that fields the use of organ into

"So clean, So lost, So beautiful."
Found That Soul single sleeve

a jabbering wall of sound in which Bradfield has to yelp over the top of to be heard. If there was any indication that over the last two records the Manic Street Preachers had lost their soul, then the title alone takes the form of their redemption. However, lines such as 'still standing here with all the scum' reconnects the band back to the audience in the same way You Love Us or Stay Beautiful did, which in their previous record they had placed a distance. At the Millennium concert in Cardiff the band had sold truckloads of t-shirts which stated 'We are the Scum Superior'.

Found That Soul was released as a single along with the more summery So Why So Sad as the album's first joint promotional singles, and the video for the song was a cheapo night vision affair mixing band performances and an assortment of young girls flicking through classic literature that the band had referenced in the past. The band had often had a tendency to launch into an album with a rush of rock 'n' roll. *Generation Terrorists* had started with the riff heavy Slash N' Burn. *Gold Against the Soul* began with the formidable

Sleepflower. *The Holy Bible* had begun with the quiet intro to Yes, but soon launched into the most devastating chorus the band had put to record. It had been during the more populist years of *Everything Must Go* and *This is My Truth...* when the band had softened their approach and eased the listener into the listening experience. Elvis Impersonator (Blackpool Pier) opened *Everything Must Go,* and the track began with a woozily strummed acoustic guitar which melted into a blistering chorus, before submerging again and ending with a rendition of Elvis Presley's American Trilogy. The song was hardly a stunning opener, in fact it was all but forgotten when the elegance of A Design For Life kicked in. *This is My Truth...* perhaps started as it meant to go on. The opening track, The Everlasting, was epic in production but ultimately an underwhelming six-minute slog. To hear the opening power chords of Found That Soul chime in in uncouth fashion caused a wave of relief and excitement from the listener.

*KNOW YOUR ENEMY* WAS A RECORD DRENCHED IN DARING and adventurism, a potent reaction to the band's recent endeavours. It contained Nicky Wire's first lead vocal, the return of Sean Moore's trumpet (last heard on Kevin Carter) and James Dean Bradfield's first full lyric on Ocean Spray. The deeply personal song was about Bradfield's mother, Sue Bradfield, and her belief in the health benefits of cranberry juice. The song opens with Manic Street Preachers photographer, Mitch Ikeda, speaking the lines 'you have very beautiful eyes... such beautiful eyes' in his native Japanese tongue. On record, Ocean Spray was a vibrantly strummed acoustic number that melted into a more aggressive posture with interludes of heavy distorted guitar. Sean Moore's lovely trumpet solo breaks the oppression somewhat. Live renditions of Ocean Spray were either an acoustic performance by a lone Bradfield or, as performed in the Karl Marx Theatre in Cuba, brash and heavy. The track was released as the record's third single and featured a video of Bradfield miming the song in a bathroom (and washing his face), Moore recording his drums and Wire playing table football and reading a newspaper.

If the band had been serious about putting up an antagonistic front then Intravenous Agnostic would have made a brilliant single. The track sees the band at their most startlingly robust and explosive and comes across as virtually effortless in its execution, both musically and lyrically. In its review of *Know Your Enemy*, the *NME* pointed out that the band had 'preserved some early flammability in the excellent Intravenous Agnostic, which despite wearing the lyrical equivalent of an "I'm With Stupid" T-shirt, offers plausible old-school thrills.'[22]

Alas, Intravenous Agnostic was not to be a single. Yet, worth noting is a trend when it comes to a third track on a Manic Street Preachers record. They seem to offer an important statement and are typically selected for single release. Bar *Generation Terrorists*' third track Born To End (which could be argued would have also made a great single) and ending the trend with *Rewind the Film*'s title song (though the song and third track, Rewind The Film, was issued with a video), every third track from a Manic Street Preachers record has been issued as a single. Beginning with the baggy funk of *Gold Against the Soul*'s 1993 single La Trisstesse Durera (Scream To A Sigh), *The Holy Bible*'s weakest song She Is Suffering, *Everything Must Go*'s Edwards' penned Kevin Carter, *This is My Truth*'s... anthem You Stole The Sun From My Heart, *Lifeblood*'s Empty Souls, *Send Away the Tigers*' redefining Your Love Alone Is Not Enough and ending with 2010's Some

"Paralysed except through my thought."
So Why So Sad single sleeve

Kind Of Nothingness from *Postcards From a Young Man*. This marks a consistent eighteen year cycle broken only by *Know Your Enemy*'s unwillingness to conform to the norms. In this sense Intravenous Agnostic could be considered a great lost Manic Street Preachers single.

I remember at the time of *Know Your Enemy*'s announcement being severely disappointed that my best friend, who was barely a fan of the band, had heard So Why So Sad on the radio before I had. He'd described the track — probably the way most radio DJs had — as sounding like a Beach Boys song. This sentiment was lodged firmly in my head when I tuned in to Jo Whiley's radio show to get my first listen. The harmonies and sleigh bells certainly give the song a sunny Beach Boys vibe, yet something darker lingers within the song. The accompanying music video perfectly translates the lingering sinister vibe. On an idyllic beach, a young boy swings a baseball bat. The band themselves play the song in a swanky cliff-side apartment, a looming structure reminiscent of a Bond villain's hideout. Children and their parents splash carefree in the surf. A white mist descends in the background. Chiseled soldiers emerge from the smoke waging a war against an unseen enemy. The families continue to soak up the rays unfazed by the carnage surrounding them, perhaps a comment on how numbing war and death had become on society. As the song ends the same young boy holds his baseball bat in anticipation, but his father throws not a baseball, but a hand grenade. Although the video itself is relatively tame (no blood, no visible death) the images of war juxtaposed against the idyllic family scenes and Speedo and bikini-clad beach bodies are stirringly affective. Although the music video came months before the events of September 11, 2001, and the pre-emptive invasion of Iraq, with the help of many other factors involved with *Know Your Enemy*, one can't help but speculate that Manic Street Preachers were commenting on past US Foreign Policy invasions.

Manic Street Preachers have always had a tendency to pull focus on one real or fictionalized member of the pop culture fraternity. The earliest example being R.P. McMurphy, the acoustic strumfest and B-side to Stay Beautiful, that used the protagonist of *One Flew Over the Cuckoo's Nest* as a means to protest capitalism and celebrate individuality. When the band released From Despair To Where as the first single from *Gold Against the Soul* they included the hammering hard rock slog of Patrick Bateman — a song that was an original first single contender — as the B-side. Despite the song's pounding metal backdrop and everything-but-the-kitchen sink approach (seriously, the song contains a sample of the Star Spangled Banner and a children's choir), it perfectly encapsulates the sinister premise and male egoism of Bret Easton Ellis' 1991 novel, *American Psycho. Everything Must Go* had also brought South African photojournalist, Kevin Carter, and abstract expressionist painter Willem de Kooning, into the spotlight. The band pushed the boundaries of who was worthy of cultural revaluation somewhat on *Lifeblood* with The Love Of Richard Nixon, a song that tried to redeem — with lines such as 'people forget China' — one of the most crooked American Presidents in history. Nicky Wire, in an interview with *Uncut* magazine

"A voice so pure, a vision so clear."
Let Robeson Sing single sleeve

recalled that song's failure: 'I can remember being in James' flat in Cardiff, hearing Jo Whiley play it on Radio 1. And I knew as soon I heard it... what the fuck have we done?'[23] Thankfully, to even things out, the band included the thoughtful Emily, a song that celebrated the life of Emily Pankhurst, one of the leaders of the Suffragette movement.

The lack of euphoric anthems on *Know Your Enemy* was striking concern upon first listen. The record's fifth track Let Robeson Sing was the first real opportunity to let Manics fans sing. Whilst a majority of *Know Your Enemy* has dated over time, Let Robeson Sing seems to have only matured, possibly due to the song's subject matter, which unlike the majority of the record expresses a positive reflection of its politics and its subject.

Paul Robeson was a black American actor, singer, and civil rights activist. He became involved in political activism with the outbreak of the Spanish Civil War (1937–1939), and gave moral support to the leftist Republican troops and the International Brigade fighting against Franco's Falange. In the era of McCarthyism, paranoia of leftist politics reached fever pitch and Robeson, along with many other artists, writers, actors and singers was blacklisted.

Whilst Let Robeson Sing might be the life of the album, it could also be an indicator of its death. Released as a single the day before the September 11, 2001, terrorist attacks the song's anti-Americanism was certainly at odds with the defiant spirit the US and its allies around the world were taking as the causes and consequences of the attack unfolded over the days, weeks and months after. For a start the song was critical of the anti-communist McCarthy era, but more importantly the fabric of the American Dream itself ('the lie of the USA'), and US Foreign Policy, which in the subsequent months after the attack was being pumped up with jingoistic flare. It might seem odd that the very Welsh Manic Street Preachers would openly sing about a disgraced commie actor from mid twentieth-century America, but Robeson's connection to Wales was intriguing. Nicky Wire pointed out that:

> There's quite a big connection. He did a film called *Proud Valley* which is based on the miners in South Wales, and he was due to come over here to perform at the Welshire Eisteddfod, which is like a celebration of culture and singing and stuff. It was when he had his passport withdrawn by the American government, so he actually sang down a telephone. He sang the Welsh National Anthem down a telephone to the Eisteddfod miners, and I've got a CD of this, which is one of the most amazing, spine-tingling things I've ever heard.[24]

Let Robeson Sing contains a lyrical premonition, as like Paul Robeson, the band in later months would also go 'to Cuba to meet Castro'.

Apart from *The Holy Bible*, which remains consistently abrasive yet strident throughout, and *Everything Must Go*, which maintains and even builds on its anthemic poignancy until the very end, Manic Street Preachers' records (at the very least prior to *Know Your Enemy*) tend to suffer from a shapeless middle section. The first tracks are often bracing emotional anthems, well-deserved singles, and poignant rockers. Take for example *Generation Terrorists*. The sheer length of the record means that by track seven, the sweet duet, Little Baby Nothing, we've already heard five of the record's seven singles. The midsection resumes with less than stunning songs such as Tennessee, Repeat (Stars And Stripes), Damn Dog and the awful acoustic re-recording of Spectators Of Suicide. The uninspired rot is broken only by the jubilant Stay Beautiful and So Dead, and only resumes its greatness when Crucifix Kiss, Methadone Pretty and Commended To Rock And Roll signify the album's concluding trifecta.

*Gold Against the Soul* is another prime example of this. The concise ten song track listing means that by track five the listener has already heard three of the record's four singles. The remainder of the record is somewhat underwhelming, an assortment of bland hard rock with only the hand-clap breakdown of Roses In The Hospital, and the queasy synth keyboard introduced in Nostalgic Pushead to liven up proceedings. Although in the case of *Gold Against the Soul* the record ends on a dud with the record's title track signalling its demise.

*This is My Truth...* also progresses in a similar vein. The first five tracks contain all four of the record's singles, starting with the slow-burning The Everlasting and ending with Tsunami. The album then enters into a meandering and navel-gazing midsection that begins with My Little Empire and I'm Not Working. This lull is barely cracked by the treacly You're Tender And You're Tired and its ill-judged whistling solo (note: I'm fine with hand-clap breakdowns, but whistling solos is pushing it), and the autumnal but ultimately forgettable Be Natural. The album doesn't pick up the slack until the graceful Black Dog On My Shoulder, and the raucous Nobody Loved You. The fact the record ends on the subdued audio experiment of S.Y.M.M. is possibly a moot point.

Manic Street Preachers' records follow a formula that is somewhat unique to the CD format. As discussed by Dai Griffiths in his deconstruction of Radiohead's *OK Computer* (1997):

> ... the CD album, arguably, placed a new emphasis on precisely the *middle* of the album, in addition to openings and endings. Another thing I remember with early CD was the bunching together of singles towards the start of the album, as though the assumption was made that the album might be switched off soon after starting.[25]

*Know Your Enemy* is no exception to this loose rule of thumb. By the time we hit track six, the breezy Year Of Purification, the listener has already experienced all the singles and all the obvious anthems they are going to get. However, unlike past records in which the mid-sections are fairly dull, samey affairs, *Know Your Enemy* does at least offer variety and eccentricity to bolster its shortcomings. A case in point, the jangly guitar and upbeat shimmering harmonies of Year Of Purification bleeds into the desolate dirge of Wattsville Blues, which subsequently heralds the arrival of the disco inflicted Miss Europa Disco Dancer. After the euro/euphoric rush it's on to the full throttle punk of Dead Martyrs, finished off by the summery His Last Painting, which along with Year Of Purification acts like the other piece of bread that sandwiches the hard-to-digest contents in the middle. The album then continues in relatively good fashion with the solid new-wave stomp of My Guernica.

The shimmering and harmonious Year Of Purification

seems standard for *Know Your Enemy*, a pointer already declared by the breezy sun drenched harmonies of So Why So Sad. Wattsville Blues, however, is another matter completely; no pointers exist at all in the entire back catalogue of the band's output. Certainly Wire's sneering vocals suit the tuneless and discordant musical accompaniment, but the overall effect of the song prompts the listener to jump for the skip button. The Wire-led B-side, Ballad Of The Bangkok Novotel, a track on the CD single of Found That Soul, might have been a better choice as it at least bristles with enough bone shaking pessimism, as opposed to Wattsville Blues lethargic slog and hateful lyrics of 'Don't want no friends' and 'Proxy fucking assholes following me'.

Despite the oddity of Miss Europa Disco Dancer it acts as a welcome and, one might add, comic reprieve from the weighty contents of *Know Your Enemy*. Though the track offers a blissful moment of euphoric joy the song is really a retort, as Bradfield explained to *Muse* magazine: 'It's criticising *Ibiza Uncovered*, *Jamaica Uncovered*, *The Villa* and *Big Brother* TV. I like the idea of people dancing to it and not realising it's stabbing them in the back.'[26]

The *NME*'s Victoria Segal offered the best description of the track, articulating that 'Miss Europa Disco Dancer is like watching *Generation Game* contestants trying to salsa', yet Segal continues that the band's intentions 'never leave you doubting their conviction.'[27] This is a fair assessment of the track; after all disco was a feature in the early lives of the band. In an episode of *All Back to Mine* — the Channel Four television series that featured musicians discussing their record collection — James Dean Bradfield recounts buying Diana Ross' disco classic My Old Piano as a young teenager, and his eternal embarrassment at his purchase being discovered by an older kid. The closing Wire-led chant of 'Brain-dead motherfucker', repeated ad-nauseam, is quite a stunning prelude and prompts the listener to imagine, or indeed engage in chanting it back mockingly at the indie disco at all the piss-heads and posers on the dance floor.

After Wattsville Blues and Miss Europa Disco Dancer there is a desire to hear the guitars go full throttle again. In some respects Dead Martyrs rings in like many rockier mid-album songs that the Manic Street Preachers place mid-record, to break what might be considered the central lull. Dead Martyrs might be considered the So Dead, Yourself or Enola/Alone of *Know Your Enemy* (as discussed above *This is My Truth...* seems to remain subdued throughout), songs that are good enough album tracks in themselves yet somehow suffer because of the surrounding songs, which are usually definitive singles or album highlights. For example, So Dead's neighbour is Stay Beautiful, whilst Yourself is sandwiched between the singles La Tristesse Durera and Life Becoming a Landslide, as is Enola/Alone, which is packed tightly between the hit singles, Kevin Carter and Everything Must Go. Dead Martyrs rings and rattles with enough punk spirit, its lyric of 'got no future' echoing The Sex Pistols God Save The Queen, but like many great Manics album tracks, it falls between the cracks of the more sturdy compositions that surround it.

Pablo Picasso's mural *Guernica,* which was completed June 1937, a year after the start of the Spanish Civil War, depicts a chaotic scene of death and violence. In an article in the *Huffington Post*, Alejandro Escalona comments that:

The chaos unfolding seems to happen in closed quarters provoking an intense feeling of oppression. There is no way out of the nightmarish cityscape. The absence of color makes the violent scene developing right before your eyes even more horrifying. The blacks, whites, and grays startle you — especially because you are used to see [sic] war images broadcasted live and in high-definition right to your living room.[28]

As Escalona later comments, *Guernica* would become an 'inconvenient masterpiece' to the US Government in their pre-emptive war on Iraq. In a press conference at the United Nations Security Council in 2003, US Secretary of State, Colin Powell, spoke about the need to go to war. Behind him a blue curtain covered up an impressive tapestry reproduction of *Guernica*. The symbolism of oppression and death was all too ironic considering what was to come.

IN THE WAKE OF 9/11 MUCH OF *KNOW YOUR ENEMY'S* ANTI-American sentiment would become redundant. But a mid-album track like My Guernica was a reminder that Manic Street Preachers could combine personal and mass trauma effectively and echo a collective mood.

My Guernica turns out to be a distorted, pounding rocker, in which James Dean Bradfield has to holler over the top of the noise in order to be heard and implores with the song itself to 'keep it together'. The track is a typical product of the record. In an interview with *Noisey*, Bradfield recalled that during *Know Your Enemy*'s recording the band 'were just laying stuff down quite quickly and not worrying about the production. And we undersold some of the songs on the record.'[29] Though startling and robust, My Guernica is perhaps one of the 'undersold' entities Bradfield was referring too. There is a more full-bodied song hiding underneath the fuzz and scratches, and a chorus as bright and shiny as Tsunami, or No Surface All Feeling feels ready to break out. The feeling is that the song is rushed and unready, with even the lyrics 'I'm blurred to bits and wired' seeming to be obscure and unreadable, though 'Alfred J Prufrock would be proud of me' gets a laugh.

The Convalescent follows, and takes *The Holy Bible* approach of cramming as many lyrics and themes into a song as possible. Again, one can't help think that Bradfield's comments about rushing through and laying down songs without a reprieve applies to The Convalescent as well. The theme of the song is that of internal thoughts and obsessions conveying themselves externally; in the case of the author, Nicky Wire, cut-outs and quotations cover the bedroom wall and his internal thoughts and obsessions in an ever-cascading collage. The beauty of The Convalescent is that the rushed musical accompaniment works with the track and feels eternally on the verge of collapse, as if the weight of the stream of consciousness lyrics ('Klaus Kinski with love of Werner Herzog') is too much to carry. The Convalescent is the sound of an aneurism, a life flashing before the author's eyes, with only a messy wall collage to show for it. The cry of 'Scream until the war is over' only amplifies the hopelessness. The song references figures in popular culture, from professional golfer, Payne Stewart 'in a death bubble', to Brian Warner, aka shock rocker Marilyn Manson's 'tasty little ass', Spanish painters Francisco Goya and Pablo Picasso to 'sweet and young' Ethiopian long-distance runner, Haile Gebreselassie, all of these characters, literally and metaphorically, share the same wall space. Wire's cataloging and collecting is well documented. Even with his own band he has kept clippings from early interviews with defunct magazines, VHS recordings of their early gigs and every single, EP and rarity.

The record then slinks into the rather sinister Royal Correspondent. Manic Street Preachers have always worn their Republicanism on their sleeve. The band's earliest photo shoots featured them pouting and posturing outside the gates of Buckingham Palace with spray painted t-shirts that read 'Death Sentence Heritage'. In 1999 the band were invited to play a free open air concert to mark the opening of the National Assembly for Wales, however, with the Queen and Prince Phillip in attendance the band declined, issuing a statement that read the '[Manics] have never and will never play in front of the monarchy.'[30] Since the storming haiku of Repeat (UK) from *Generation Terrorists* called for a violent overthrow of Britain's monarchy, the band have issued only a number of anti-monarchical retorts. Their rather crass cover of McCarthy's Charles Windsor called for the decapitation of the first in line to the throne and a revolution to overthrow corrupt business and the media. Perhaps the most glorious and righteous anti-monarchy song recorded by the band was nestled on the B-side of Kevin Carter. First Republic was a brash and, for its era — that of Cool Britannia — a daring proclamation of the band's anti-monarchy stance. The song hopes that the monarchy has done the right thing and 'guillotined' their own heads before the rabble do it for them. Royal Correspondent is certainly anti-monarchy ('They're inbred baby just like you'), but it takes its fury out on the hoity media who cavort with and appease the royal family rather than denounce the Windsors themselves.

Though somewhat of a throwaway, Epicentre contains a few poignant moments and works as a calmer counterpiece to the lyrical stream of consciousness of The Convalescent and My Guernica. The song momentarily breaks down into a wonderful sonic experiment interlude of looped harmonies that proclaim 'Happy black days here's the summer', something that wouldn't make sense until the release of Let Robeson Sing and the accompanying B-side Masking Tape, which featured the experimental interlude in full. Epicentre seems to be a comment on keeping oneself medicated and physically intact. Lines such as 'I worship the painkiller' recall Wire's humorous admittance to camera after exiting the stage during the Cardiff Millennium concert that the high he was feeling at that moment was akin to 'four paracetamol', the most drugs he'd ever taken.

Baby Elian appears to be desperately searching for a coherent tune. The awkwardly composed verses seem like a deliberate attempt by the band to sabotage a song that could have built on the singalong quality of Let Robeson Sing and given the later part of the album a potential single, or a rousing moment at the very least, though the opening chime of chorus ('kidnapped to the promised land') does eventually allow for the song to break through and become somewhat anthemic. Again, this appears to be a victim of rushed production. Nonetheless, the song is critical to the record. Baby Elian sets the stage for the band's jaunt to Cuba and the meeting with Fidel Castro, who gets praised for not just sitting 'on a rocking chair' whilst the Cuban Revolution was under construction. The song took on the subject of Elian González, a young boy who in 1999 along with his mother and her boyfriend, attempted to flee Cuba for Miami. His mother tragically died during the crossing and González was placed with his maternal relatives in Miami. The family sought to keep him in the United States, but González's father, who remained in Cuba, wanted him returned. In June 2000, agents from the US Border Patrol Tactical Unit (BORTAC) raided González's relatives' home in Miami and returned him to his father in Cuba.

American photographer Alan Diaz, who had been on the scene at the time of the raid, took an iconic photo of a BORTAC agent pointing an assault rifle at a terrified González, which won the Pulitzer Prize for Breaking News Photography. Baby Elian was distinctly pro-Cuban and outright anti-American, referring to the USA as 'the devil's playground'. After the band's concert at the Karl Marx Theatre, the Cuban newspaper *Granma* singled out Baby Elian as 'a dart thrown against the manipulation of consciences by a culture that, from a position of hegemony, aims to make the world a uniform place.'[31]

The album concludes with Freedom Of Speech Won't Feed My Children, a bristling and savage attack on celebrity endorsed causes and as Brendan Reid put it in his review for *Pitchfork* 'a warning against complacency, self-righteousness, and lax activism.'[32] Though you wouldn't know it, the track features My Bloody Valentine guitarist, Kevin Shields. The song acts as a sort of perverted flipside to If You Tolerate This Your Children Will Be Next and challenged the failed liberalism of the Dalai Lama, The Beastie Boys, and Hollywood actor Richard Gere, all accessories in the Free Tibet campaign that was at the time a highly fashionable cause for celebrities to latch onto. Ultimately it fails as a protest song, raising unfocused points about the side effects of globalization that 'Just brings heart disease and bootleg clothing'. As concluding tracks go it sits with *Gold Against the Soul*'s weak eponymous song, and S.Y.M.M from *This is My Truth...* which like Freedom Of Speech Won't Feed My Children ends the record in unfocused protest.

Except the album doesn't end there, and for that one could be thankful. As sprawling as *Know Your Enemy* is it still has another surprise. A few minutes of silence, in which the record's disappointments and triumphs settle on the listener's ears, leads to a hidden track, a cover of British indie darlings McCarthy's jangly and highly politicized track We Are All Bourgeois Now. The oddity of the song in comparison to the previous sixteen tracks of Americanized punk/disco/west coast rock is startling, and, despite the joyous conclusion to the record, also demeans the previous listening experience somewhat. Manic Street Preachers tried to summarize all the working class rage, the evils of war, imperialism, capitalism and the futility of modern western society over an entire album that clocks in at over seventy-five minutes. Yet the band's effortless cover of We Are All Bourgeois Now manages all this in just over four minutes, in fact the single lyric 'Once there was class war, but not any longer' pretty much summarizes the defeatist politics of *Know Your Enemy*. The band's cover of McCarthy begs the question from the listener: what was the point in everything that came before?

The ultimate point of *Know Your Enemy* was to forge a different version of the Manic Street Preachers that was almost completely set apart from their previous incarnations. After the disappearance of Richey Edwards, the band may have continued in a sonically different direction, discarding many of their obtuse traits, yet the presence of Edwards was always felt. It was obvious that the band wanted to acknowledge his legacy by the inclusion of his lyrics on *Everything Must Go*, whilst the melancholia of *This is My Truth...* felt like a delayed reaction to the loss of Edwards. Songs such as Nobody Loved You were obvious paeans to their missing friend. *Know Your Enemy* felt like they had finally shaken themselves out of the daydream and created a version of themselves, respectful of, yet free of Edwards' presence, something that was unique to them as a three-piece band. Their sense of being provocative was more focused on the political aspects of their brand of socialism. It was a more unified experience. This is why *Know Your Enemy* feels so different in almost every respect and perhaps why the critical and fan responses were muddled. They had done so many things one way for so long that the change in direction was too abrupt for listeners to fully take stock.

# OUR MANICS IN HAVANA

THE FIRST CONCERT TO LAUNCH MANIC STREET PREACHERS'
much anticipated fifth album, *This is My Truth Tell Me Yours*,
took place on September 15" 1998, at the Kettering Arena, an
English backwater town in Northamptonshire. This was part
of a small primary tour of towns the band had rarely, if ever,
played. This was an opportunity for them to bring the music
to the type of provincial setting they themselves had grown up
in. The *NME* described the Kettering gig as uninspiring: 'Even
a crowd-surfing wheelchair (I kid you not) doesn't inspire
him (James) beyond an apparently functional performance.
Likewise, Nicky ends up sitting down towards the end of the
newly ironic sounding Faster.'[33] No doubt to the glitter and
feather boa-clad kids moshing upfront this performance
lingers in the mind many years after. Yet surely, as early
proclamations stated, Manic Street Preachers wanted the
world, now they had it in their grasp the decision to launch
their most anticipated record, one that already contained
a number one hit single, in a small provincial sports arena
boggles the mind.

Or does it? The band has reminisced about their early
exposure to live music. As youths desperate to see their
favourite bands they would often have to travel far and wide
to catch a live performance from Echo and the Bunnymen, The
Alarm or Adam and the Ants. The small town of Blackwood

never received the mainstream bands of the time, so journeys to nearby Swansea, Cardiff, Bath or Bristol were regular. By the time I saw the band live for the best time at the massive Birmingham NEC on the full arena tour a few months after the Kettering gig, ambition was back in swing, and the embrace of being a critically acclaimed and publicly-adored band had enlivened their performance. A year later, on the eve of the millennium, the Manic Street Preachers would reach the epoch of this ambition with their sold-out concert at Cardiff's Millennium Stadium.

Ten years earlier they'd stated world domination or nothing. As the clock ticked to a new era, the world seemed ready to embrace them.

The controversial launch of *Know Your Enemy* at the Karl Marx Theatre in Havana, Cuba, would encapsulate some of the ideals behind the Kettering gig and the subsequent tour of smaller towns and venues. By performing in front of an audience that rarely gets to see the likes of Manic Street Preachers trundle through town, the band was bringing the music to an audience unaccustomed to such a high profile act. However, instead of a backwater in the middle of England, the Manic Street Preachers decided to launch in one of the world's last remaining socialist outposts.

In the run-up to the concert, James Dean Bradfield shed some light on the decision to play in Cuba that seemed to be more about going up against American cultural imperialism than openly sponsoring Cuba's socialism, as he discussed with Simon Price in the *Guardian* newspaper: 'Cuba is an example that everything doesn't have to be Americanised.'[34] Nicky Wire followed up James' comment with: 'it's just that Cuba for me is the last great symbol that really fights against the Americanisation of the world.'[35] In the run-up to a record release (especially one that sounded so Americanized), it may not have been wise to rankle an entire potential record buying market, but the Manic Street Preachers, who had never quite connected to a mass North American audience, really had nothing to lose, and so with the help of Neath MP, Peter Hain, then a member of the foreign office, who convinced his Cuban contacts that the band members were a left-leaning bunch, they ventured to where no western band had been in decades. In fact the Manic Street Preachers were among only a number of artists that had visited Cuba since the Revolution. A revue show featuring the likes of Billy Joel, Rita Coolidge, Kris Kristofferson and Weather Report played in Havana in 1979, the year after Castro permitted a list of state-approved western bands to be played on radio, including Jimi Hendrix and The Rolling Stones, who would venture to play in Cuba in 2016. The most familiar jaunt to a communist state by a pop sensation in modern memory was Wham's 1985 excursion to the People's Republic of China, thawing tensions with pop diplomacy at the height of the Cold War.

Of course I didn't attend. Not many actual fans did, most of the UK fanbase had to tune into the televised documentary, read about the meeting with Castro in the music press or later buy the live recording when it was issued as the video and DVD, *Louder Than War*. Yet the performance was possibly one of the band's most celebrated. Performing in front of a few thousand Cubans, who had paid the equivalent of seventeen pence to attend the gig, the sheer joviality of band and audience was a wonder to behold. In this context the band brought with it no history or baggage onto the stage. They played familiar and well-rehearsed songs to a zealous audience who had never heard a single note of the Manic Street Preachers' back catalogue. In the band's case, most live

"Went to Cuba to meet Castro." *Louder Than War* DVD sleeve

occasions contained a general unease between them and the audience, and a perception by both on how the event should proceed. Requested heckles of 'Play Revol!' or 'Sleepflower!' are common features of a gig, much to the dismay of the band, and the knowing audience who know how unlikely it would be to ever hear the much-loathed (by the band anyway) Revol live, but scream for it anyway. I recall a moment when seeing the band at the Nottingham Arena during the *Lifeblood* tour of 2004 and being severely disappointed when, instead of playing Faster with the usual fierce gusto one expects, the band chose to perform a jazzy acoustic rendition. What should have been a moment of mosh-inducing catharsis, especially considering the less than lively tracks on *Lifeblood*, was reduced to schmaltz. Indeed the calm acceptance in which Manic Street Preachers were embraced by the Cuban youth was disorientating, as Simon Price noted in his review for the *Guardian*: 'For the first number, there's polite applause.

For the second, isolated dancing. After the third, there's a technical hitch and a long pause. The delay meets with total silence — no sarcastic handclaps, no chanting, just respectful patience.'[36] If this technical hitch had occurred anywhere in the United Kingdom or Europe the band would have met with a damming chorus of sarcastic chants, jeers and boos.

YET THE BAND WERE TREATED AS DEITIES BY THE CUBAN press and the public. The only uncomfortable moment was the slightly awkward meeting with Cuba's then leader Fidel Castro. The band looked like schoolboy prizewinners in the presence of the stately Castro, laughing as Castro made jokes about the noise of rock music not being 'louder than war'. History carries a lot of weight, and depending on your political allegiances, and which side of the ideological divide you fell on, Castro's was at times the heaviest load in the modern era. Perhaps the band's quiet socialism did not extend quite as far as bloody revolution. Quoted in the *Japan Times* a few months later, Nicky Wire reflected on the experience:

We were disturbed and inspired in equal measures: There was the ever-present symbol of the gun and all this overbearing civic symbolism. The TV channels were very corny and tightly controlled, but on the other hand the people were not disenfranchised from their own culture, they were eager to point out their own culture. They are very sociable, hospitable people. We ate with ordinary families. When we bought clothes, they would discuss with us where the material came from, the labor costs, etc. It wasn't just a case of sanitized McDonald's-style transactions and consumerism.[37]

However, in the wake of the experience, Wire's reflections changed. And when Fidel Castro stepped down as Cuba's president in 2008, and power was handed to his brother, Raul Castro, Wire, in an interview with *Uncut* magazine, saw problems emerging.

> It's like the runt of the family is going to get the job. When that happens it's always bad news. I was impressed by Fidel, when we played in Cuba 2001, in the sense that he was so well briefed and so on it. Cuba was what I expected. Communism is a failure — I'm fully aware of that. I just wanted to see the one place it still operates. People go on about the poverty in Cuba, but the life expectancy is 79.4 years. That's not poverty. Africa is poverty. And the education — everyone I met spoke English. I was impressed by certain parts, but the reality of a communist state was... a reality. There were elements of it that were absolutely shit.[38]

When Manic Street Preachers played Cuba the country was still suffering from the imposed US embargo. In the post 9/11 environment Cuba would still come under scrutiny, but the Cubans were no longer the US bogeymen. The proposed threat of communism — a political ideology- would be replaced with jihadist Islamic extremism, a twisted interpretation of religious ideology. Progress between the United States and Cuba began to improve in July 2015 when diplomatic relations between the two nations were restored via an agreement negotiated by President Barack Obama and Raul Castro. Though the trade embargo remained in place, it was seen as a step towards normalizing relations. Though steps taken by Obama's successor, Donald Trump, saw a reversal of these negotiations as policy dictated to 'Make America Great Again' and thus discount any peaceful coexistence with unpopular regimes.

Though hardly any fans were in attendance, the Manic Street Preachers' jaunt to Cuba did mean something to those back home, especially newer fans such as myself who had been denied, just by not being aware at the time, the outrageous and outspoken controversies of the first three albums. In some respects, the Cuba gig was *our* Horse and Groom 1989, *our* Reading 92, *our* Glastonbury 94, *our* Astoria 94. The gig rolled up Richey carving '4 Real' into his arm, Wire's deathwish to Michael Stipe, Bradfield in a balaclava screaming through Faster on *Top of the Pops*, and the band's disintegration in Thailand all into one palatable statement. All this past behaviour was a faded memory to long-time fans, or a curious blip in the band's early history as their demure from *Everything Must Go* onwards was that of dignified elders of British alternative rock. Even if the record didn't match up with the ambition, the trip to Cuba was a bold statement. It gave fans who were simply too young or shielded from the band's initial incarnation an opportunity to join with a group who stood for *something*. The politics were unfashionable and quaint in the wake of Francis Fukuyama's declaration a decade earlier that the end of the Cold War was also the end of history. Free market neoliberalism was now the dominant political idea. Whatever the band's own beliefs, communism had lost the ideology war. Retreating into an alternative reality for an entire record was an unwise strategy. The flip flop of music genres contained on *Know Your Enemy* was also a lesson learnt, though one not fully comprehended until after *Lifeblood*. Upon the band's return to commercial good graces in 2007 with *Send Away the Tigers*, Nicky Wire virtually dismissed the era of *Know Your Enemy* and, with it, embraced his own failure. Signing off from the *Uncut* magazine interview, Wire declared with Fukuyama-like certainty that 'I am a failed communist — but I think that's a good thing, because communism is a failure.'[39]

# THE B-SIDES OF *KNOW YOUR ENEMY* AND THE ALTERNATIVE HISTORY OF MANIC STREET PREACHERS

THERE IS A THIRD INCARNATION OF THE MANIC STREET Preachers which goes beyond the simple divide of the 'with Richey' and 'post-Richey' eras. It is a hidden identity, a subconsciousness where the band has been free to express and experiment with failure and success without as much critical judgment that often befalls the records. Manic Street Preachers have always been a quality B-sides band, though this facet of their career has often been overlooked. However, the same musical adventurism, lyrical intelligence and production value that is witnessed throughout the band's album tracks applies to the B-sides as well. Indeed, here the band chose to hide these compositions from a mainstream audience, instead leaving them for the fans to discover.

On B-sides such as Dead Yankee Drawl, Us Against You, Sculpture Of Man, First Republic and Dead Passive the band show a more radical political awareness than might be witnessed so blatantly on the main albums. On songs such as Bored Out Of My Mind, Hibernation, Donkeys, Just A Kid and Too Cold Here show a willingness to explore a revealing and reflective self-awareness. B-sides also provide an output to cover songs by major influences or adversaries, such as their versions of McCarthy's Charles Windsor, The Happy Mondays'

Wrote For Luck, Alice Cooper's Under My Wheels, and The Clash's Train In Vain. They also give the band an opportunity to experiment with sound and genre. Witness the audio flushes and weird instrumentation on B-sides Love Torn Us Under, Comfort Comes, Dead Trees And Traffic Islands and Locust Valley.

This diversity can be witnessed throughout their single output, but as a microcosm of this, one need only look to the B-sides included on the CD single of Kevin Carter. The first track after Kevin Carter, Horses Under Starlight, is glorious and has the distinction of being the band's very first instrumental, a bold statement from a band who place intelligent lyricism at the forefront of their work. The personal reflection is witnessed on the song Sepia, a blatant and beautiful melancholic paean to the missing Richey Edwards that translates the author's internal anguish and pain ('I'm bleeding inside I manage to keep it all in'), towards a notion that is poignant, yet also positive. The band's radical politics are on full display with the last track, First Republic, a punk retort to the royal family that wonderfully calls for the revolting rabble to 'play in burnt out palace ruins' and hopes the Queen, as noted earlier, has guillotined her own head before the chanting masses have broken through the palace gates. The song, though snarky and juvenile, harks back to their bolder anti-monarch statements on *Generation Terrorists*, such as Repeat UK and the early B-side, We Her Majesty's Prisoners.


TO MY MIND, THE CONSISTENCY IN QUALITY THAT MANIC Street Preachers devoted to B-sides places them in the same arena as the definitive B-sides band, Oasis. Their 1998 B-sides compilation, *The Masterplan*, sold just as many copies as their main albums despite many of the band's fans already owning most of the songs across various single formats. Songs that were originally B-sides such as Acquiesce, Talk Tonight, Half The World Away and Round Are Way became staples of Oasis live shows. Although arguably Manic Street Preachers have not achieved that kind of success with any one particular B-side, the work taken as a whole offers insights that are not as apparent on the main records.

Manic Street Preachers have often used B-sides as pointers towards their next major recordings, signalling a change in musical style or lyrical concerns. The most apparent example is Comfort Comes, nestled on the CD version of Life Becoming A Landslide, the last single to be taken from the smooth sounds of *Gold Against the Soul*. Comfort Comes is something of a revelation when taken in the context of its lead single and the polished mother record it comes from. Tight compacted drums, strained metallic vocal, regimented guitar. The song has the sense of being crushed under its own weight at any second. Strangely it doesn't, but instead keeps steadily marching onwards. In many ways Comfort Comes acts as, not just a predecessor to *The Holy Bible* as a whole, but also as a musical template for *The Holy Bible*'s explosive first single Faster. Only the song's lyrical content differs. Comfort Comes regards the author's search for a companion who will offer soothing words ('need someone to nurse me') and tend to all needs without complaint. Faster on the other hand deals in an almost shocking need to find absolute solitude, and self-reliance in oneself ('I am stronger than Mensa').

Pointers to *Know Your Enemy*'s bombastic sound actually lay on the very first single from its predecessor, *This is My Truth Tell Me Yours*. Prologue To History and Montana/Autumn/78 were B-sides featured on If You Tolerate This Your

Children Will Be Next. Both tracks contained a more raucous and distorted production value, courtesy of producer Greg Haver, who would produce and engineer Royal Correspondent and Freedom Of Speech Won't Feed My Children from *Know Your Enemy*, as well as engineer *Lifeblood* and play drums on both James Dean Bradfield and Nicky Wire's solo projects. Prologue To History was the most apparent departure from the mother record: tumbling drums, a clipped shouted vocal and jabbing keyboards, it was also crammed with cultural figures, such as British middle distance runner Steve Ovett, Happy Mondays' vocalist Shaun Ryder and even the band's own Richey Edwards as the 'poet who can't play guitar'. It signifies the everything-but-the-kitchen-sink sonics of *Know Your Enemy*'s The Convalescent and Found That Soul.

The B-side Socialist Serenade, included on You Stole The Sun From My Heart, the third single from *This is My Truth...* also pointed towards the band's return to their more radical roots and direct political analysis that would come to fruition on *Know Your Enemy*. The song features a pounding looped drumbeat, jagged guitar, and lyrics that quite clumsily take down the so-called socialist ethics of the New Labour government with lines like: 'Change your name to New, Forget the fucking Labour'. The track denounces the introduction of student loans and paying 'for the privilege' of education and goes on to lambast Tony Blair's political celebrity and his regular holidays to sun-drenched Tuscany.

Another bridge towards the *Know Your Enemy* era was included on Tsunami, the fourth and final single from *This is My Truth...*. The song Buildings For Dead People was a fuzzed-up mutant dirge of The Beatles song, Revolution. Its vague lyrics might not stand up to much scrutiny with references to the NHS and 'from the womb into the tomb' policy of lifelong healthcare, but as with Comfort Comes which led the way to a more militaristic sound, the music that accompanies Buildings For Dead People lays the shaky groundwork for *Know Your Enemy*'s key tracks like My Guernica and Dead Martyrs. After the Millennium gig in Cardiff, the peak of the band's immense popularity, Manic Street Preachers hunkered down with the intention on creating a new and distinct version of themselves and their sound.

IN FACT IT WAS IN THE SAME WEEK OF THE MILLENNIUM concert that the band set out a new agenda. The standalone single, The Masses Against The Classes, was a blast of pre-*Generation Terrorists* era punk rock that began with a sample of Noam Chomsky and finished with Bradfield bellowing an Albert Camus quote. Whilst the band had tested the patience of their widening audience with songs about the Spanish Civil War and a Welsh villages going underwater, The Masses Against The Classes was a call to arms and an opportunity to redefine themselves and refine their audience somewhat in preparation for *Know Your Enemy*.

With Masses Against The Classes, the band scored their second number one. The single featured two new tracks: the thumping and discordant Close My Eyes included a personal critique of the last few years of the Manic Street Preachers' embracing of their popularity and the price that has on one's sanity. The author's disillusion with fame is seen in lines such as 'Sign some papers and then they are my friends', which could be alluded to signing autographs for fans or record contracts and publishing deals, either one carries its burdens. This critique of post-fame is something that crops up repeatedly on Manic Street Preachers songs. It would appear the weight of being in a successful band was a double edged sword. The most obvious example being You Stole The Sun From My Heart, in which the author has 'gotta stop smiling', because it makes them approachable and content, but even if this is the case, the line 'I love you all the same' seems to indicate that the burdens are worth it. Despite not being written by Manic Street Preachers, the full throttle cover of Chuck Berry's boisterous Rock And Roll Music offered a surging blast of good time rock 'n' roll that counteracted the disillusionment of Close My Eyes and set the band towards their re-affiliation with rock 'n' roll.

It would be another thirteen months before the band dropped the double-single release of Found That Soul and So Why So Sad, with both tracks being a diverse sampler for the forthcoming *Know Your Enemy*. Found That Soul was a shambolic blast that gave an example of the rockier aspects to be found on the record, such as My Guernica, Intravenous Agnostic and Dead Martyrs, whilst So Why So Sad was more breezy and tender, reflecting songs such as Ocean Spray, Year Of Purification, and His Last Painting. If the A-sides were a surprise to fans, old and new, then the B-sides were something to behold. So Why So Sad featured a mesmerising remix of the track by Australian act The Avalanches (who scored a world hit with their album *Since I Left You* in 2000). The other new track was Pedestal, kicking off with a continuously building wall of drums and guitar, before the chorus breaks through like a whirlwind.

The CD single of Found That Soul also featured two new tracks. Locust Valley contained a darkly sinister verse that jostles for dominance with one of the most breezy and carefree choruses Manic Street Preachers had ever set to record ('I don't need it, I don't fear it'). However, if *Know Your*

*Enemy* was committed to a new approach in sound and style then The Ballad Of The Bangkok Novotel was the epitome of this. The Ballad Of The Bangkok Novotel was a full blown punk rock detonation that saw Nicky Wire taking charge of lead vocals. The song was reminiscent of Sid Vicious' raucous interpretation of Frank

"To breathe only air where life should be." Ocean Spray single sleeve

Sinatra's My Way. The track throws the listener back to the madness of *The Holy Bible* era and the band's 1994 spring tour of Thailand where strains in the band dynamic, and Edwards' conditions began to have serious repercussions. Lyrics such as 'Four sickly boys are losing resistance' sum up the band's poor health and personal disintegration at the time. Wire's lyricism and almost helpless delivery reflects the homesickness and despair of that era. The track encapsulates the experience of being lost and alone in a foreign climate, eating strange foods ('mini sized apples') and longing for home whilst trapped in an unfamiliar hotel room. The track also signifies the beginning of Wire's Mark E. Smith-meets-Lou Reed vocal contributions to the band. Although Wire had provided backing vocals on an early B-side, Sorrow 16, a song contained as a B-side on the Motown Junk single, and had sang a duet with Bradfield on *This is My Truth*'s My Little Empire, Ballad Of The Bangkok Novotel provided the band's audience with a taste of what was to come from Wire's future solo endeavours and the *Know Your Enemy* track Wattsville Blues. From this point on Wire would not be far from the microphone.

The more sombre Ocean Spray, and third single from *Know Your Enemy*, spread its B-sides across two different formats, CD and cassette tape, which would be the last cassette the band would release in a format that was on the verge of being obsolete. The cassette single featured the angry and menacing number Little Trolls, a retort against writer and critic AA Gill, who in 1998 had penned a scathing attack on the Welsh nation in the *Sunday Times*, describing its people as 'loquacious, dissemblers, immoral liars, stunted, bigoted, dark, ugly, pugnacious little trolls.'[40] These remarks saw Gill reported to the Press Complaints Commission. Little Trolls contains some of Manic Street Preachers most vitriolic lyrics. As retaliations go, Little Trolls packs a punch and slams Gill in the most heinous ways as a 'Retarded ugly balding old man', but it's a great shame that the track was left adrift on a declining format. Not only is it spiteful and sneering, but Gill may never have known that he was the subject of such a much deserved retort.

The CD version of Ocean Spray featured the tracks Groundhog Days and Just A Kid. Groundhog Days begins as a gentle acoustic lament, similar in mood to an earlier B-side Hibernation. However, the track suddenly explodes into a blistering anthem when the chorus kicks in. It also features another Wire vocal contribution, a spoken word monologue that quotes Bill Murray's character, Phil Connors' dialogue from the 1993 film *Groundhog Day* ('Is this what you do with eternity, I've killed myself so many times I don't exist anymore'). Manic Street Preachers use the film's repetitive narrative as a metaphor for the repetition and mundane attributes of modern existence.

If Groundhog Days talked of the disillusionment brought

on by adulthood then the other new track, Just A Kid talked of a longing to return to childhood. With its thumping drums and discordant guitar Just A Kid was similar in sound to Pedestal, yet the lyrical content harked back to *The Holy Bible*'s only real innocent plea, This Is Yesterday. Similarities exist in the use of sky and sunshine ('I stare at the sky' from This Is Yesterday, 'so afraid of the sky' from Just A Kid) as metaphors for youthful independence and endless days of summer. Whilst This Is Yesterday offers a melancholic perspective of childhood, it is the melancholia of adult experience that is tainted. The grown-up author of This Is Yesterday wishes to return back to innocence to rid themselves of being an adult. Just A Kid reflects on a positive and carefree existence ('A kid kicking around with no worries'), but is more frightening, as the cynicism of adulthood, seems to be haunting the author even as a child. This lyrical theme of being young once again, is something of a staple Manic Street Preachers topic that would be repeated on the 2014 song Rewind The Film. In that particular song, the author wants to continue to revisit and relive parts of his youth from records, books and home movies, ('I'd love to see my joy, my friends').

The last single from *Know Your Enemy* was Let Robeson Sing the wonderful lament to the activist and actor, Paul Robeson. The album's only true singalong moment. The CD version contained Masking Tape and a cover of the traditional song Didn't My Lord Deliver Daniel, which Paul Robeson himself had once sung. Masking Tape was yet again another song about being a Manic Street Preacher, this time taking on the form of the bonds of friendship, of the unbreakable 'masking tape that holds our lives together'. On the 12″ vinyl sat one of the more interesting of the band's B-sides: Fear Of Motion, a bristling short number, with rising and fading synths. In terms of pointing towards the future, as Manic Street Preachers B-sides tend to suggest, Fear Of Motion indicated that their experimentation with synthetic sound was imminent. This trend continued after *Know Your Enemy*, although not B-sides as such, but on the additional tracks from the 2002 greatest hits package *Forever Delayed*: Door To The River and There By The Grace Of God also pointed towards more subtle future recordings.

Let Robeson Sing also contains perhaps the most successful remix up to this point in the Manic Street Preachers back catalogue. The Stone Roses' vocalist Ian Brown provides a mesmerising reworking of the song that allows James Dean Bradfield's vocals to echo and ascend, whilst the remix drops the Robeson spoken word moment, it is replaced with a Brown midsection rap. This might sound slightly absurd, but remember, the band members were keen rap fans, especially the political commentary of Public Enemy, from an early age, and so far they had yet to incorporate this influence into their very white rock 'n' roll music. It's also worth pointing out that *Know Your Enemy*'s diverse mix of styles and sounds lends itself to remix much better than past records. The band attracted many remix collaborators such as David Holmes, The Chemical Brothers, and Cornelius, but the only real successful adaptations of the Manics sound came from Stealth Sonic Orchestra's lush and sweeping versions of Motorcycle Emptiness, Design For Life, and The Everlasting, which all appeared as B-sides.

Though it doesn't quite correspond with the quality of the *Generation Terrorists* B-sides, by far the best era until *Send Away the Tigers* came along with a collection of rollicking anthems worthy of inclusion on the main record (Boxes And Lists, Anorexic Rodin, Welcome To The Deadzone, to name but a few), the B-sides of the *Know Your Enemy* era showcase the band ploughing ahead with the experimentation shown on the mother album. In some respects there is even a case to be made for tracks such as Ballad Of The Bangkok Novotel, Pedestal, Groundhog Days and Just A Kid as worthy editions to *Know Your Enemy* as a whole. They certainly display more guile and anthemic quality than say the clunky Wattsville Blues, the mellow His Last Painting or the sinister Royal Correspondent. The daring and attention given to B-sides during *Know Your Enemy*'s campaign, shows that the band was in the midst of a creative spell. In a move that was unprecedented for the band (or maybe that should be the record company who presumably made the decision) the B-sides of *Know Your Enemy* were issued as a standalone compilation CD entitled *Know Our B-Sides* exclusively for the Japanese market. In many respects the band were for once proclaiming that the tracks hidden on single formats were worthy of a coherent compilation.

# CONSUMING *KNOW YOUR ENEMY*

THE RELEASE OF KNOW YOUR ENEMY IN 2001 ARRIVED AT the height of my own Manic Street Preachers fanaticism and consumption of their music and lyrics. By this point, *Everything Must Go* and *This is My Truth...* had been staples on my CD player for a few years, joined by *Generation Terrorists* and *The Holy Bible*. I had collected most of the band's previous singles, EPs, and rarities on CD, vinyl, and the odd cassette tape by raiding secondhand record shops and rummaging through dusty piles of vinyl at record fairs. I'd seen the band live a number of times, often in cities that required some travel and having to sleep in mates' cars overnight and journey back home the next day. I purchased the *NME* and *Melody Maker* weekly, and brought the monthly music magazines *Q* and *Select*. All these publications featured Manic Street Preachers on a regular basis. I was hooked into any morsel of information about the band. (By the time *Know Your Enemy* was released, *Melody Maker* had merged with the *NME*, while *Select*, as with Britpop, had folded by 2000.)

*Know Your Enemy* also came at a transitional point in how I was consuming music. The internet was still relatively new to me, a slow and noisy dial-up connection that was costly to be on for any length of time was all I had. The band's embryonic website and chat forums were out of reach, so most of my excitement for the record was generated by listening to Jo

Whiley, Steve Lamacq and Mark and Lard's BBC Radio One shows (and of course reading the *NME*). YouTube, Myspace, Facebook or Spotify didn't exist, so most of *Know Your Enemy*'s actual music was first heard on radio or television. In some ways *Know Your Enemy* was the last album (or the last Manic Street Preachers album for sure) that I heard by obsessively holding my ear to the radio waiting in anticipation with the tape deck set to record as soon as the first chords chimed in. Jo Whiley I think first played the singles, I saw the music video to So Why So Sad on Ant and Dec's *SMTV*.

I bought the album from HMV on the day of release and ran home for the first full listen. As with *This is My Truth…*, I opened the CD inlay to read along with the lyrics as the record was playing, and marvel at the handsomeness of the band in the inlay photographs. The lyrics of *Know Your Enemy* were reproduced in Wire's scrawled and unclear handwriting on sheets of photocopied lined paper. One could see the edits, the verses that were cut or repositioned, and the possible titles that were discarded (My Guernica's title option was Subconscious Abstraction). It was meant to demonstrate to the listener an instinctive and relaxed approach to the recording process. It even showed direction. Across from the title of Miss Europa Disco Dancer, Wire had written and circled 'Lets Go-Disco'. No band photos, or photography of any kind for that matter was included. This was alarming. Manic Street Preachers record sleeves were like mini manifestos. Quotations were scattered around the inlay, dedications to underdog causes and lost friends, pictures and collage. The best example of this is *The Holy Bible*, a beautifully produced booklet of religious, sexual and political imagery that matched the music perfectly. Even the sleeve for *Everything Must Go*, a moment when they were at their most nondescript, contained imagery and dedications that set the mind in motion and showed from where they came.

Getting into the actual listening of the record, I recall being mildly disappointed. Reading and memorising the lyrics of a Manic Street Preachers record was a crucial component of the listening experience. I found, at least initially, that *Know Your Enemy* contained no real quotable statements, no big choruses, which was at first discouraging. Eventually, this facet of the album actually gave it a longer lifespan and obtuse lyrics ('Narcissism so lonely so live by the sea') eventually became some of my favourites. In the subsequent weeks there was always something new to discover in the more indigestible tracks like Baby Elian, Royal Correspondent and Epicentre, which seeped in on repeated listens. It took a few weeks to absorb the contents. One actually had to make the effort with this record.

I wasn't the only one to experience this strange record on these terms. *Know Your Enemy* was perplexing for many listeners. That it sits somewhere towards the bottom of most fan-made lists is hardly a surprise. It is not an easy record to love.


NOW THAT WE HAVE DELVED INTO THE MUSICAL DEPTHS of *Know Your Enemy* I want to explore responses to the record, not from a critical perspective but from fans that actually do (kind of) like the record. I made contact via Twitter with a number of fans of the Manic Street Preachers. The response was good, though one might assume that a discussion on *The Holy Bible* or *Everything Must Go* would have generated more participation. However as the discussion of *Know Your Enemy* continued, it became clear there were points raised that simply would never have come up on a discussion about any other Manic Street Preachers record.

Gareth is a teacher living in London with his wife and young children and an avid fan of the Manic Street Preachers since when he was a teenager growing up in Market Harborough in the East Midlands. He formed the punk/pop band Tokyo Beatbox (later to be called Beat Fiction), with a bunch of like-minded lads in an effort to replicate some of Manic Street Preachers' lyrical intelligence with a more youthful punk vigour. His first reactions to the album reveal something of the transitory times in which it was released.

Tellingly (given that Nicky Wire ended up getting embroiled in an argument about illegal downloading — rightly pointing out that Napster and the like were not charities and would be selling shares in the near future) I'd heard most of the album before it came out. Not through illegal downloads per se but via digital recordings of live performances, radio previews etc which meant that one way or another ten or more tracks were already out there to listen to. This was a first for me and served to dilute the occasion of the album's release. I think by this point in my fandom I would've loved it whatever it was: I'd decided they were the best band on Earth and would fiercely defend anything and everything they did.

Gareth came to this record in a similar way to myself. A few of the songs had been previewed on radio and the band had been given an unprecedented double appearance on *Top of the Pops* to play the single release of So Why So Sad and Found That Soul. Commercially speaking, the band were at the height of their powers and anticipation for *Know Your Enemy* was feverish among fans and indeed, as Gareth points out, anything the band did at this point would have been greeted with rapture. Gareth continues:

> For me it was all part of a contrivance that many of us readily bought into. Millions of fans (like me) had got into the Manics via their commercially successful stuff, but having heard the first three albums, were desperate to be part of something along those lines: something more interesting, raw, provocative. I was only ten when *Generation Terrorists* came out, so it's not like people my age had ignored them in their early days — we were just too young (this is something Simon Price articulates really well) and it felt as though *Know Your Enemy* was our chance to have a version of *that* band — political, loud, naïve but *ours*. As I say, a key word here is contrivance: we were twenty by this time, wanting to feel sixteen; the Manics were thirty and wanted to sound like they were twenty-five. As much as I loved *Know Your Enemy* in my heart of hearts I never quite got over that sense of contrivance — we were all looking for something that wasn't quite there.

Gareth makes an excellent point. Being a 'new fan' of the band myself, it was a shock to discover Manic Street Preachers had a past as glam punk provocateurs, who dissed John Lennon in song (at the time untouchable in the wake of Oasis' acknowledgement of his and The Beatles influence on their own music), wished death pay a visit to R.E.M.'s Michael Stipe with AIDS, quoted Marx, Ginsberg, Plath, Nietzsche, wore eyeliner and ladies' blouses, and toyed with homoeroticism in the era of loutish lad rock. Whilst the band had left the lipstick

behind during *Everything Must Go* and *This is My Truth*...,
fans, old and new, held this era in rose-tinted esteem. Fans of
the band could point out that whilst the current incarnation
of the band were guilty of wearing beige khakis from Gap
and carried a little podgy weight around the gut, there was
once this radical version that existed when the band were
gorgeous, slim and spiteful. *Know Your Enemy* gave the newer
fans something to gloat about, and offered a similar version to
the original incarnation of the band, minus the makeup and
mother's blouses.

Gareth also makes some valid points about the way
listeners were consuming music. The emergence of illegal
downloading and file-sharing websites like Napster were
under great scrutiny from the industry. Bands and artists,
most famously Metallica, took the matter to court and fans
that had downloaded records illegally were being prosecuted
for theft by the band's record company. Mega-selling acts and
fey indie concerns felt their livelihood was being robbed.

Mark is a session drummer, songwriter and sound engineer
in Northern Ireland. He has worked in the studio with bands
like Snow Patrol, Editors and Kasabian. He also plays and
writes songs with the band White Male Actors. He has seen
Manic Street Preachers live a staggering twenty-seven times.
Mark's initial response to *Know Your Enemy* was similar to
both Gareth's and my own. Mark explains:

Uncharacteristically for me I read along with the lyrics
while listening to the album for the first time and I found
them to be incredibly disjointed and actually ludicrous in
parts. Now, I think a trend with Manics songs is for the
lyrics to sound quite disjointed with unusual phrasing (I
suspect because the lyrical writing process and the music

writing process is done separately and by separate people) and most of the time it works for me but in this instance I found myself being jolted from the music in a way that wasn't positive. I maintain to this day that lyrically this is Wire's worst hour.

I'm in some disagreement with Mark on the album's lyrical direction. *Lifeblood* is, in my opinion, Wire's worst hour, lyrically speaking: a dreary, meandering, and incoherent set of lyrics that seem to want to address big themes, but get stuck in the author's throat. *Lifeblood* is saved by the quite beautiful musical compositions. Like Mark, I also studied the lyrics closely and was gravely disappointed by the lack of quotable lyrics and mosh-inducing anthems that were the band's bread and butter. Yet, as discussed, in the end this is what gave *Know Your Enemy* its longevity. The lyrical content of Intravenous Agnostic is a startling series of prized couplets, whilst The Convalescent crams as much cultural reference points in as all songs on *Generation Terrorists* combined (well, not quite, but you get the point). The lyrical themes are let down somewhat by the lazy Wattsville Blues and the quick to place the blame of Freedom Of Speech Won't Feed My Children, yet overall, and taking in the context of the album's launch in Cuba, *Know Your Enemy* is an arcane mash-up of sound and culture. Continues Mark:

Musically I was very impressed with some of the songs on first listen — Found That Soul is an incredible album opener and even songs like Ocean Spray, while somewhat delicate, took on a more aggressive stance thanks to the extremely raw production which was a serious departure from the two albums previously. My Guernica is a standout track for me that is rarely mentioned by any Manics fan which I find perplexing. However, despite the raw and aggressive approach that this album takes I believe it is the 'softer' tracks such as Baby Elian, Royal Correspondent, Epicentre and Ocean Spray which truly help bolster the credentials of the album.

I'm in agreement with Mark with the musical achievements on display. The band had stretched themselves greatly when it came to sound and production, and beginnings of this could be heard on *This is My Truth...*, with the studio experimentation of tracks such as S.Y.M.M. and I'm Not Working, but *Know Your Enemy* took it to its logical conclusion. Each track has a sonic refinement that is either deliberately placed or is a symptom of the recording conditions. It is interesting to hear an audio engineer's perspective on *Know Your Enemy* as it is the most 'engineered' album by the band up until this point (*Lifeblood* would possibly surpass it in its glacial sheen). The band made a point of never second-guessing themselves and strived to capture each recording of the songs in its first attempt — hence the rough demo version of Let Robeson Sing actually ends up being the completed album version. The record is smothered in post-production fuzz, tweaks and weird audio interludes (see Dead Martyrs and Epicentre as prime examples). The organic and rustic sonics of *Everything Must Go* and *This is My Truth...* were a thing of the past that wouldn't really return until *Send Away the Tigers.*

Lizzie lives in Brighton and at the time of speaking is completing her PhD in Gender Studies. What is interesting is that she became a Manic Street Preachers fan quite a while after *Know Your Enemy* was released. A rare thing when considering the band bemused most of their hardcore fans and probably didn't pick up many new ones in *Know Your Enemy*'s wake. She explains:

> *Know Your Enemy* came out before I was a bonafide Manics fan, I'd bought You Stole the Sun From My Heart when it came out on CD single and by the time *Know Your Enemy* came out I was an avid *Q Magazine* reader and remember distinctly standing for *ages* in my local record shop trying to decide whether or not to buy *Know Your Enemy* on the strength of the *Q* review, given that I had liked You Stole the Sun... but hated the B-side — Socialist Serenade. Ultimately, I walked away with some other *Q*-lauded release from that week.

As previously discussed, a kind of sonic bridge to *Know Your Enemy* was the song Socialist Serenade, a track that fused scratchy guitar and a political takedown of the New Labour era of Champagne Socialism. Presumably at this point Lizzie would have loathed *Know Your Enemy*. She continues:

> The change for me with that album began when I heard them play Let Robeson Sing at the O2 with Gruff Rhys and his vocals on that performance just took it to a whole new place. I decided I'd been too quick to judge.

In my own opinion, Let Robeson Sing was a highlight of *Know Your Enemy*. Listening to the live version that Lizzie mentions it's clear to see why she was so taken with it. The track's raw production, an approach the band choose to take, actually improves the overall feel of the song. It shimmers instead of soars. However, the performance with Gruff Rhys at the O2 gives the song a tender feel. Rhys' voice reaches higher than Bradfield's and the song, in this case does soar. With this experience, Lizzie returned to the band.

> I went back to *Know Your Enemy* shortly after the O2 and began putting one or two tracks from the second half of the album onto my regular rotation playlists. Freedom Of Speech Won't Feed My Children, and Epicentre ended up being my 'route in' and I began putting the album on heavier and heavier repeat.

Typically, these two tracks which alongside My Guernica, are the result of what James Dean Bradfield referred to as rushed compositions. I find it interesting that these songs were Lizzie's introduction to the record as a whole, as for the most part they were not standout tracks. Nonetheless, repeated listens opened them up.

> Ultimately, it was after the release of *Rewind the Film* that I finally fell in love with the album as a whole and as of *right now* my favourite tracks are The Convalescent and Royal Correspondent. Lyrically, I think The Convalescent is possibly Wire's best ever. I love the quiet reflection and the way it evokes that claustrophobic head space of rattling round a house unable to muster energy enough to break out and alternately celebrating and lamenting that. Royal Correspondent is very enjoyable both musically and lyrically — I love that it's good old fashioned vitriolic Manics.

The Convalescent is indeed a lyrical triumph for Wire, and the subject (domestication and obsessive collecting) was something he'd been trying to communicate for a while. The

B-side, Mr. Carbohydrate is an example, as is My Little Empire. On both occasions, Wire had seemed defeated by this, but, as Lizzie points out, The Convalescent seems to celebrate it.

Lizzie's path and reaction to *Know Your Enemy* is very interesting and reminds me of my own build-up to listening to *The Holy Bible*. After solidly absorbing *Everything Must Go*, *Generation Terrorists* and *Gold Against the Soul*, *The Holy Bible* seemed like a daunting task. The history surrounding the record seemed at first to get in the way of the listening experience. I didn't fully appreciate or understand the record until after *This is My Truth...* had been released, and I had seen the band live for the first time on the supporting tour. And, as discussed above, whilst the band were embracing a more reserved aesthetic, it became satisfying to go back to a more brutal version of Manic Street Preachers and during the subsequent years hear snippets of *The Holy Bible* intermingled with the populist songs during live shows.

And it is now to the live experience of *Know Your Enemy* we turn to. With the record being plugged as their most vital statement since *Generation Terrorists*, and the most vitriolic since *The Holy Bible*, it was only right that the band's live shows would reflect this. The album launch at the Karl Marx Theatre in Havana was not a fair indication of the excitement they could generate. In the presence of an unfamiliar audience and a revered Socialist dictator, the band played it fairly straight, without too much rock 'n' roll provocation and certainly no Wire in a dress. The Cuban audience on the other hand lapped up the performance, using it as an opportunity to dance and headbang to their heart's content. Mark recalls, the *Know Your Enemy* tour was full of energy with far more intimacy than previous encounters, a consequence of their loss, as pointed out earlier by Bradfield, of a million record buyers. This nevertheless made it a more magical experience for those that clung on. As Mark explains:

I was lucky enough to see them a few times on the tour. In Manchester, Dublin and Irvine. The Dublin show was absolutely insane and the band even commented about how much energy they had and how fast they were physically playing the songs that night. The performances at each show were incredibly energetic and the band really seemed invigorated. It was also nice to see the band playing in smaller theatres and venues than on the *This is My Truth...* tour.

Mark's comments are similar to those of Gareth's when it comes to the band's new found live energy during this period. Mark says:

It's one of the best gigs I've ever been to. It was breathtakingly good, especially as songs like Wattsville Blues and Miss Europa Disco Dancer (clearly not album highlights) were extraordinary live novelties (Nicky is singing! James is playing a double-necked guitar! A disco ball descended from the rafters!) Found That Soul the perfect live opener and an ace statement of intent. I remember James getting spiky and defensive about So Why So Sad ('If you don't like this it's because your record collection isn't as good as mine.')

Decently recorded live CDR bootlegs (a sign of the times) confirm that the band was indeed playing some truly wild shows. Even the disco track Miss Europa Disco Dancer took on a punk rock defiance. From Gareth's and Mark's recollection of the live shows, the interaction between band and audience was at an all-time high. It was clear that the tracks from *Know Your Enemy* translated into a live setting quite easily and strengthened the band's back catalogue even more.

As discussed, *Know Your Enemy* felt like the record that the newer fans desperately needed. We had all heard about the controversies and read archived interviews of the band's bold statements and rhetoric against other bands and popular figures. We had acquired secondhand copies or reissues of You Love Us (Heavenly Version), Motown Junk, New Art Riot, Theme From M*A*S*H and Revol, fragments of the band's preposterous days of snarky incitements. It was fun to look back on these records and see images of the band from less than a decade before, dressed in stenciled blouses, white skinny jeans, roughly applied eyeliner. Yet when the band hit the stage, or appeared on television with the likes of Jools Holland or Chris Evans one had to admit those days, even though they were a grasp away, were over. Manic Street Preachers were no longer the snotty brats of the punk rock revival. Yet *Know Your Enemy* seemed to offer an opportunity to relive those halcyon days with the current incarnation of the band. Gareth continues this point:

> I guess it crystallises my earlier point about CONTRIVANCE. There was no real context for this album as there had been for the previous five — no one in hospital, no one missing, no one self harming, no one promising to sell sixteen million and split, no one trying to follow up a No. 1, so they had to contrive a context for the record and Cuba became that misguided, yet interesting endeavour. The actual gig is so sweet (plants for crash barriers, local trumpet player) that I'm always glad they did it, as I said,

this was a narrative we were all buying into to recreate our own slice of '91, ten years too late.

Mark continues this point:

As Gareth pointed out above, there was an element of contrivance throughout parts of the album and that tended to work less well on the more raucous tracks than they did on the quieter tracks which is surprising. I also wouldn't be too quick to slate the album based on the presence of this contrivance because I believe *Send Away the Tigers* and *Postcards From a Young Man* to be dripping with contrivance — an attempt to unashamedly conquer the charts and while it was deemed successful to a certain extent in these cases it was less so with *Know Your Enemy*. There are a myriad of possibilities for this but I believe that Manics fans are extremely protective of the band's political past and any attempt to revisit those days with any level of sustained intent is often met with hostility and incredulity.

I'm in full agreement with Gareth and Mark's comments on contrivance, and this point that will be discussed further in the conclusion. Since the release of *Send Away the Tigers*, Manic Street Preachers have been far more open about musically referencing their past records and intentionally evoking that nostalgia. What should be pointed out here is after a few unstable years of attempting to redefine themselves and explore new sounds with *Know Your Enemy* and *Lifeblood*, Manic Street Preachers simply returned to what they did, and what they were best known for: rollicking stadium rock tinged with melancholia and a sense of the theatrical. Nicky Wire summed up their approach:

The Manic Street Preachers have been through a process of destroying what we are. All great bands do that but ever since *Everything Must Go* and *This is My Truth* we've been trying to reduce ourselves to a pile of rubble. So, for *Send Away the Tigers*, we've been listening back to *Everything Must Go* and even the youthful idealism of *Generation Terrorists*, placing ourselves back at being eighteen or twenty-one again.[41]

On the one hand it was a relief to have the band slip on the rock 'n' roll jacket so easily and find that it still fit so well, but in retrospect *Send Away the Tigers* marks a phase in the band's career where they opted to actively please the audience, make stadium-friendly rock that subtly let political commentary slip through the backdoor, and refer back to their past either in sound and style or by reissuing past glories.

# IN THE AFTERMATH OF
## *KNOW YOUR ENEMY*

*KNOW YOUR ENEMY* WAS SUCH A BEWILDERING EXPERIENCE for both fans and the band themselves that the only plausible way to follow it up was to pull together assemblages of Manic Street Preachers' past hit singles and delve into some hard-to-find obscurities. Post *Know your Enemy*, there were two retrospectives of the band's career. The greatest hits collection, *Forever Delayed* (2002), brought together the band's best known and most successful singles. A reminder that, despite the weird schism just witnessed, the band had recorded numerous chart friendly anthems. Mark Beaumont reviewing the compilation in the *NME* complained that the collection 'wasted a valuable opportunity to retell their heartbreaking and triumphant story and diluted their vibrant technicolor history into a stodgy grey mulch.'[42] This was mostly a correct assessment in that it painted out a lot of the band's political output in favour of more populist selections. Omitted were such fan favourites as the blistering Revol, the punchy PCP and the timeless Slash 'N' Burn. Complaints were also made at the disharmony of the compilation's track listing. No chronological sequencing, no divide of the 'with' and 'post' Richey eras. The band had tried to encapsulate an entire career in seemingly random strokes. For a new listener, it would have appeared that the band had written and recorded a number of politically

"Paralysis through analysis."
*Forever Delayed* album sleeve

worthy rock anthems, but without the context of eras and incarnations it was hard to secure a legacy for the hit singles as a whole.

*Lipstick Traces: A Secret History of Manic Street Preachers* (2002) was a compilation of B-sides, rarities and cover versions. Titled after Greil Marcus's seminal music text, *Lipstick Traces: A Secret History of the 20th Century*, for whose reissue Nicky Wire had written the foreword, the whole package was aimed more towards the diehard long term fans than *Forever Delayed.* It was the flipside of the hits package, an esoteric mash-up that signified an alternative narrative for the band, and contained some real curios such as the acoustic haiku cover of Nirvana's Been A Son. The compilation was a mess of random sequencing, but for this compilation it mattered little. All of these songs were intended for obsessive fan consumption. One of the tracks included on *Lipstick Traces* that drew the most attention was Judge Yr'self, a powerful remnant of the post *Holy Bible* era but pre-Richey disappearance, intended for inclusion as the main theme song to the big-budget Sylvester Stallone film *Judge Dredd* (1995), which very likely would have brought the band some serious wider acclaim.

Judge Yr'self's lyrical theme was an astute revision of Faster, a kind of 'self-rule through self-mutilation' as Taylor Parks put it in *The Quietus*. Parks continues to explain that Judge Yr'self was the 'the product of a mind running out of road.'[43]

Due to the sparse lyrics and Nietzschean attitude it is a fair assumption to make that Edwards had reduced his thoughts down only to the most incisive.

"The majesty, the majesty."
*Lipstick Traces* album sleeve

Both these compilation albums contained new or never before heard tracks which pulled away from the diverse, rough and ready sound of *Know Your Enemy* and opted instead for cleaner, crisper production ethics. For example, the single used to push the hits package, the autumnal There By The Grace Of God, experimented with a sparse electronic sound. It seemed as if Manic Street Preachers were now abandoning their punkish, guitar driven sound in favour of subdued electronica. Confusingly the new track, 4 Ever Delayed, was left off its near-namesake album and instead was included alongside the obscurities on *Lipstick Traces*. Like There By The Grace Of God, 4 Ever Delayed infused synths as an undercurrent of the song, yet was far more anthemic than There By The Grace Of God. The only other new song included on *Forever Delayed* was the achingly beautiful Door To The River, which was considered as a single contender to promote the collection. The song was originally recorded during the *Know Your Enemy* sessions, but couldn't find its place within that record's wild compositions.

Then came the band's seventh album, *Lifeblood*, and for once in the entire history of Manic Street Preachers they intentionally stripped themselves of colour, verve and swagger, hiding behind a sheen of exquisite production and clean white sleeve design. At the time of the release of *Know Your Enemy* the world was in a virtual calm. Brendan Reid's review in *Pitchfork* laid this out:

1. We are rich.
2. There are no wars or anything (real wars, that is).
3. Ummm. Very little continental drift going on (that's probably normal).
4. Somewhere, the president's daughter is 'like, totally wasted' right now.
   So what are these Manic Street Preachers bitching about?[44]

Indeed one could argue that the band had released an intensely volatile and political album at a time that was apolitical and without mass conflict, at least not in the west. Though anti-globalization protests had rocked Seattle in November 1999, during the World Trade Organization conference, it was the terrorist attacks of September 11, 2001 and the subsequent war in Iraq and Afghanistan that threw the world into a colossal period of unrest. With their new record, a political entity such as Manic Street Preachers could have taken the cues of *Know Your Enemy* and run with them, loading each and every verse with political commentary and denouncing the escapades (or 'crusades') of George W. Bush and Tony Blair. We could have had a British version of Green Day's epic 2004 operatic punk record, *American Idiot* — a year before that record set the world alight. *Lifeblood* was not to be that record.

The band was complacent in *Lifeblood*'s pop subtlety. Nicky Wire stated to Dorian Lynskey in an interview in the *Guardian*: 'I don't mind if people think this album is quite coffee-table, I see that as a compliment. I think *White Flag* by Dido is a brilliant record.'[45]

As shocking as that statement is, *Lifeblood* was the pop record the Manic Street Preachers had been building towards (or threatening to make, depending on your perception of pop music) for many years. There was

"Make life slower."
*Lifeblood* album sleeve

perhaps a hint of *Lifeblood*'s future existence in Manic Street Preachers' collaboration with dance outfit 808 State on the sublime and dreamy 1996 song Lopez.

The album's second and final single, Empty Souls led with a beautiful piano motif but was a hollow comment of the events of September 11, with 'Collapsing like the twin towers. Falling down like April showers' changed to 'Collapsing like dying flowers' for the radio edit. Lyrically the record was also fairly dull. Whimsical, half-baked personal sentiments had replaced political posturing. Yet musically it was a huge leap from the band's previous sounds, Nicky Wire called it 'a mature record... elegiac pop.'[46] Instead of the abrasive clatter of *Know Your Enemy*, *Lifeblood* was a spacious mosaic of synthesisers, strings, keyboards and lush harmonics. The record allowed for wide breathing spaces within the textures of the songs, whereas the band's tradition was to cram every millisecond of song with as much riff and meaning as one could muster, *Know Your Enemy* being a prime example. The approach to *Lifeblood* was also different from previous records, particularly in contrast to *Know Your Enemy*'s quick-fire and fluid approach. One of *Lifeblood*'s producers and its engineer, Greg Haver, recalls that the *Know Your Enemy* recording sessions were certainly 'Less stressful!' but that '*Lifeblood* was a very hands on record for me that started with me doing the demos and some work in New York with Tony Visconti.'[47]

Despite the dab hand of Visconti, the record didn't fare as well commercially as previous endeavours. However, *Lifeblood*'s musical calm was also not helped by an impending ten year anniversary retrospective of *The Holy Bible*. Released only a month afterwards, a digitally re-mastered rendering of the record also featured an unheard, yet often discussed, US mix, exclusive bonus tracks, a DVD containing a new documentary on the making of the album, and the music videos for the record's singles Faster, Revol and She Is Suffering. The tenth anniversary re-release of *The Holy Bible* reminded fans and critics of what Manic Street Preachers were lyrically, musically, aesthetically and politically capable of. *Lifeblood* seemed to wither away under the colossal retrospective. In the 2015 documentary *No Manifesto*, the whole history of *Lifeblood* is covered in less than five minutes. James Dean Bradfield's definition of the record and the era is summarized (or dismissed) as a 'strange anomaly'. Although *Lifeblood* certainly feels unlike any Manic Street Preacher record, the subtlety in sound and autumnal melancholia achieved by the musical compositions should be applauded.

WITH WHAT WAS THE PERCEIVED FAILURE OF *KNOW YOUR Enemy* and *Lifeblood* it felt like the band had very little choice in the direction to take. A period of reflection was imminent and much needed. In 2005, the band embarked on the Past/

Present/Future Tour, a series of arena concerts that allowed the band to play the hits alongside more obscure tracks from their back catalogue. This would be the last live performances from the band for at least two years. As a way to reconnect with the fans and promote the tour the band issued a free download only EP called *God Save the Manics*, which featured three brand new, or possibly reconstituted, B-sides that were destined for *Lifeblood*'s nonexistent third single. All three songs contain pointers to future endeavours. The first track A Secret Society reworks the driving riff from Joy Division's She's Lost Control and adds an explosive and shouty chorus that points towards *Send Away the Tiger*'s more rockier moments. The James Dean Bradfield penned Firefight acts as a lead up to Bradfield's 2005 solo record, *The Great Western*, in which songwriting duties would fall solely upon his shoulders. The most interesting song was Picturesque which was a composite of two Richey Edwards' penned lyrics. This was something that most fans of the band thought they would never hear: writings set to record from the much-discussed binder that Edwards had handed to the band prior to his disappearance. The lyrics from Picturesque would be given another airing on *Journal for Plague Lovers* in the songs All Is Vanity ('I would prefer no choice') and Doors Slowly Closing ('Crucifixion the easy life'). The image used as a sleeve design for *God Save the Manics* featured a black and white photo of a glammed-up Nicky Wire from the *Generation Terrorists* era snarling at the camera like Sid Vicious.

When touring duties ceased, James Dean Bradfield and Nicky Wire both recorded solo records. Bradfield's *The Great Western* was a traditional and soulful blend of ballads and gospel-tinged shimmering rock standards. The only Manic-like moment came on the record's first single and lead track,

That's No Way To Tell A Lie. Beginning with stabbing electric guitar, the track soon softened with the inclusion of some 'sha-la-la-la' backing vocals and wondrous hand claps.

*The Great Western* was an interesting artifact in that it contained the first collection of Bradfield penned lyrics — with help from his novelist friend John Niven on some tracks. There had already been a taste of what Bradfield could achieve lyrically on *Know Your Enemy* with Ocean Spray, but here was a full body of work that pointed towards Bradfield as more than a hard-riffing conduit for Edwards and Wire's words. The record showed a soulfulness and tenderness rarely seen on a Manic Street Preachers record. Songs such as An English Gentlemen and Still A Long Way To Go were remarkably different, whilst Bradfield's cover of Momus' To See A Friend In Tears was actually tear-inducing.

WIRE'S SOLO ENDEAVOUR SHOWCASED THE SHABBIER, less commercial aspects of the Manic Street Preachers' influences. Entitled *I Killed the Zeitgeist*, it was a raw collection of sneering (the only way Wire can really 'sing' is to 'sneer') straight-up punk and lo-fi indie rock. As with some of the earlier Wire voiced compositions, the vocalization was certainly not to everyone's taste. A review by *The Final Word* described Wire's voice as 'a blunt instrument, lacking range or expression but somehow articulating the point more effectively for the inarticulacy of the voice.'[48] Yet with the shambolic musical accompaniment, Wire's *Zeitgeist* actually worked very well. Wire described to *Uncut* the experience of writing and recording the record as:

an outpouring. It was going to be a poetry album, but I

turned up at the studio and did four songs in two days. It was effortless just in the sense that I had no expectations. When I made it, I wasn't even going to release it.[49]

Unlike his role within the band, Wire wrote all the music, and songs like I Killed The Zeitgeist, Break My Heart Slowly, Shining Path and Goodbye Suicide, were revelations in musical accomplishment. In the wake of these records, Wire would become a more active composer for the Manic Street Preachers. Sean Moore's solo record was notable by its absence.

The idea that the band could one day fragment was perhaps the catalyst for a renewed vigour upon their return in 2007. It seemed almost shocking that the Manic Street Preachers could release one of their most life-affirming and upbeat singles as they approached their eighth record and almost their twentieth year as a band. Your Love Alone Is Not Enough was a magical moment in their career. Perhaps it was the solo records that invigorated the band's creative spirit. Producer and Manic Street Preachers collaborator, Greg Haver, who was recruited as drummer on both Bradfield and Wire's solo projects shares this view:

They were very different experiences for me. I was drummer on both records and a member of Nicky Wire's Secret Society (and our four legendary gigs). We had a lot of fun with Nick putting that record and shows together. My drumming on *The Great Western* is probably the best I will ever submit to record as James really brought the best out of my playing and pushed me into areas I had never tried before. There was certainly a change in energy after the solo albums and tours, I think they realised that they needed each other! [50]

"Trade all your heroes in for ghosts." Your Love Alone Is Not Enough single sleeve

Featuring the sweet vocals of The Cardigans' Nina Persson, Your Love Alone was a duet made in heaven and something the Manic Street Preachers had been trying to accomplish ever since Little Baby Nothing, which featured the spryly sweet vocals of porn actress Traci Lords, and Black Holes For The Young, which featured the genteel tones of Sophie Ellis-Bextor (then of indie darlings, Theaudience). Your Love Alone... shimmered and sparkled like no other Manic Street Preachers song had in recent memory. Unlike the vast majority of the band's back catalogue, this one came with a musical composition written by Nicky Wire.

After the success of the single, anticipation for the album, *Send Away the Tigers* (2007) was high. *Send Away the Tigers* re-launched the Manic Street Preachers back into the popular consciousness. Featuring blasts of Guns N' Roses style rock, soaring anthems and glittering punk, the album typified the band's traditional sound with a vigour that had been lost on the experimentations of *Lifeblood*, but also featured songs that harked back to *Generation Terrorists* and *Gold Against the Soul*. The album's lyrics were a mixture of political commentary and personal reflection. Indian Summer, for example was based on similar subject matter as The Everlasting and This Is Yesterday, that of a longing for a return to youth, but its musical a complement was uplifting in a way the band had never managed to fully capture before.

"This one's for the freaks." *Send Away the Tigers* album sleeve

The more political aspects of the record came in the form of Imperial Bodybags, which contained affective imagery of war and 'Children wrapped in homemade flags', whilst Rendition added a twist of dark humour to the horrific acts of torture, or rendition, implemented by the American government by wishing such outspoken liberals as Jack Lemmon were still alive to speak out against the traumas of war and injustice. Even the hidden cover version of former hate target, John Lennon's Working Class Hero reflected on the band's class roots. Though *Know Your Enemy* and *Lifeblood* had been fairly well-received, there was a collective sigh of relief in the music press for *Send Away the Tigers*. The *NME* called it 'easily the best thing the band have released since 1996. Concise and focused, bristling with political ire and with unabashedly

"Wish me some luck as you wave goodbye to me."
*Journal for Plague Lovers* album sleeve

lowbrow salutes to the trio's guiltiest musical pleasures.'[51] Whilst *Pop Matters* acknowledged that the band had looked back at their history to look forward in order to 'regain those glory days of the previous decade. In a move that seems ridiculously obvious and yet shockingly evolved.'[52]

The Manic Street Preachers' next record, *Journal for Plague Lovers* (2009) could have laid waste to the critical good graces and new found appreciation for the band. The record used the remaining lyrics that Richey Edwards had handed to his band mates prior to his disappearance. For this momentous project, the band recruited Steve Albini, the famed producer of Nirvana's startling yet sombre 1993 masterpiece, *In Utero*.

After the success of *Send Away the Tigers*, it could have been a *Know Your Enemy* style disaster. Wire acknowledged this in an interview with Alex Petridis in the *Guardian* newspaper: 'This album could seriously damage us in a commercial sense... Already, supermarkets won't accept the album cover, which I am really startled at.'[53] The album cover art that Wire was referring to was a Jenny Saville painting that featured a stark close-up of a young girl looking bruised and beaten. It was certainly fitting that *Journal for Plague Lovers* featured a Saville piece. Most commentators saw the resemblance between the girl on the sleeve art and a haunted Edwards. In actual fact the timing of *Journal for Plague Lovers* couldn't have been better. With the success of *Send Away the Tigers,* the band could not be charged by critics with attempting to kick-start a stalling career by making reference to past glories.

*Journal for Plague Lovers* was conceived by James Dean Bradfield. He said:

> I'd been looking at Richey's lyrics anyway... I'd always imagine putting music to them, then I'd get a bit scared and put them back in a drawer. But this time I'd looked at them and it was the first time I couldn't stop turning the pages and I was getting ideas and stuff.[54]

Upon completion Wire stated that he didn't even want the record to be released: 'Let's just fucking dig a hole and bury it and make it even more of an art statement, say we've made this great album, but it's just too much to give away.'[55] Bradfield, ever the working class grafter, refused to hear of it. Many reviewers compared it to *The Holy Bible*, most were also cautious to list its numerable contrasts. Whilst the production value of *The Holy Bible* was stark and oppressively suffocating with only rare glimpses of beauty, *Journal for Plague Lovers* offered plenty of moments of subtle splendour, light, and even humour. Whereas songs such as She Bathed Herself In A Bath Of Bleach and Doors Closing Slowly were as dark and disturbing as anything on *The Holy Bible*, songs such as Jackie Collins Existential Question Time and Me And Stephen Hawking had some cracking one-liners embedded in the lyrics ('Oh, mummy what's a Sex Pistol?' was a particular fave). No official singles were released from the record, which meant *Journal for Plague Lovers* had to be consumed by the listener as a singular artistic statement of Edwards' lyrical intent.

Manic Street Preachers were in the midst of a huge creative spark. After the blip of *Journal for Plague Lovers*, The courteous nature of the band (possibly over-courteous in the wake of *Journal for Plague Lovers*) continued on their next record, *Postcards From a Young Man*, a collection of solid anthems, every one of which had hit single potential. Nicky Wire attempted to explain in *Wales Online* the weird schism that led to *Postcards From a Young Man*: 'There are two versions of this band maybe. There's the "Journal" and "Bible" version and then there's this version. That over the top hysterical dignity, that flash of intelligence.'[56] The band made no secret of their ambitions. James Dean Bradfield stated to the *NME* that they were 'going for big radio hits on this one', and proclaimed the record their 'one last shot at mass communication.'[57] An album designed to appease a mass audience. Wire followed up this comment with his own justification in an interview with *Digital Spy*: 'We've always been about infiltrating the mainstream. It was a conscious decision this time to want to hear ourselves on the radio.'[58] The riffs borrowed heavily from Guns N' Roses (the track A Billion Balconies Facing The Sun even featured former Guns N' Roses bassist Duff

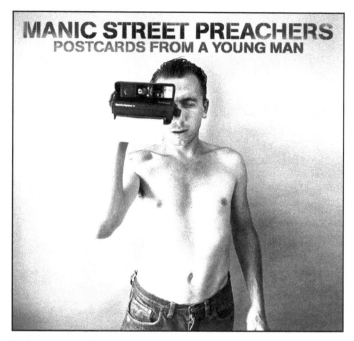

"We're so post-modern, we're so post everything."
*Postcards From a Young Man* album sleeve

McKagan), and whilst the nature of the band harked back to the *Generation Terrorists* era of ambition and attitude, the overall ideal seemed to be pandering to the audience on the audience's terms, as opposed to the band's own. This attempt at scoring hits and appeasing the masses appeared to backfire with the band's lowest charting singles in decades.

The first single, (It's Not War) Just The End Of Love was startlingly simplistic yet with its string-drenched arrangement certainly ambitious. The song's strings were a direct sample from Chic's 1978 single Everybody Dance, which was also sampled by UK pop band, Steps, on their 1995 single Stomp.

Incidentally, Manic Street Preachers and Steps had been involved in a Blur/Oasis style chart battle for the top spot in 1998 with If You Tolerate This.... and Steps' One For Sorrow (surely a Manics song title contender). The promotional video for (It's Not War) Just The End Of Love featured fellow Welshman Michael Sheen and actress Anna Friel as two international chess players (Sheen plays under the Welsh flag, Friel under the Soviet) who then discard their game and mount the chess table to kiss passionately. Despite heavy radio play and numerous television appearances to promote the single, (It's Not War) Just the End Of Love failed to make the UK top twenty, stalling at number twenty-eight.

The winter of 2010 was, for a large majority of young people in the United Kingdom, a winter of discontent. Students rallied in their thousands against the Conservative/ Liberal Democrat coalition government's decision to allow universities to increase their tuition fees to up to nine thousand pounds a year. The prospect of the working-to-lower middle class sending their offspring to university was looking almost impossible. The protests that transpired were for the most part peaceful, but the sense that a whole generation's future had been torn apart provoked anger that only echoed the disillusion with capitalism and corruption that was being felt the world over. Across the Atlantic, Occupy Wall Street sit-ins in New York City were taking place. Well-known left-leaning writers and journalists joined the protesting hordes to offer their support and even give impromptu lectures on the need for protest and political alternatives. Noam Chomsky, Chris Hedges and Slavoj Žižek all attended the sit-ins and informed the protestors on capitalism gone rogue and what could be done about it. Occupy Wall Street was soundtracked by members of political stalwarts Rage Against the Machine, whose brand of outspoken rap/rock/funk had been railing against the mechanisms of globalized power for decades.

When the political situation required them most, our own stalwarts of socialism were to be found kitted-out in sharp suits and ties plugging their new single on *Strictly Come Dancing*. The lack of any real political commentary from the band during this time was notable. A Conservative/Liberal Democrat Coalition seemed absurd. Though both parties occupied a centre ground and believed in a free market neoliberalism, the Lib Dems of 2010 were pushing an almost leftist agenda that included free university tuition for all. From the 2010 election onwards, if felt like the United Kingdom had decided to experiment with a form of sitcom-style politics in which everyone collectively played the straight man to the comedy of errors dealt out by the Coalition. Nicky Wire, talking in the *NME*, even commented on Lib Dem Deputy Prime Minister, Nick Clegg, in this context: 'He just reminds me of David Brent, he's a terrible motivational speaker, real third rate.'[59]

Outside of their music and lyrics, the Manic Street Preachers have never been comfortable with grand political gestures, with only a few rare exceptions. In 1994 they'd played at the massive Carnival Against the Nazis, and in 1997, they'd performed at Anfield Stadium in support of Justice for Hillborough. The band's audience are well attuned to this schism between what they hear on record and what they see on-stage, or in the press, i.e. the music and lyrics always spoke louder than the things they talked about in interviews or wore on-stage, and this was more apparent in the absence of Richey Edwards. However, their decision to play *Strictly Come Dancing* during the most politically turbulent times in recent British history was perverse, even for a band whose

"A fitting end to your end." Some Kind Of Nothingness single sleeve

sense of irony is well intact and equally acknowledged. The song they performed that night was Some Kind Of Nothingness, a gospel-tinged duet with Echo and the Bunnymen' frontman Ian McCulloch, though McCulloch was absent from the performance which left Bradfield to duet with himself. The fact that Some Kind Of Nothingness was the band's lowest charting single in the UK in nearly twenty years, reaching number forty-four, meaning that the band had missed the top forty for the first time since 1991, should have set alarm bells ringing.

The lack of success for the single, despite the mass exposure, proved that the band simply could not appease the majority of their own fans, as well as a majority of ordinary music fans, or live up to the idea of 'mass communication' that *Postcards From a Young Man*, the record Some Kind Of Nothingness came from, wished to achieve. Nicky Wire admitted in an interview with *Absolute Radio* how he 'was quite distraught that Some Kind Of Nothingness, had missed the top forty. I was gutted.'[60] The performance on *Strictly Come Dancing* signalled what I thought was the end of my own love affair with the Manic Street Preachers. When they played Cuba in 2001, it was against the grain of popular political sentiment at the time. Yet it was so audacious that even in the face of much adversity it felt like an immense accomplishment. Their turn on *Strictly Come Dancing* also felt out of tune with the political climate but for all the wrong reasons.

In a 2011 interview with the *Guardian*, Wire had stated that:

We won't be releasing a record for two or three years but we'll be trying hard to make one. Can we do something good enough so we keep going? We've got to do something that impresses us. We've got to do something gigantic.[61]

Early interviews from the band talked of a sprawling triple vinyl opus titled *70 songs of Hatred and Failure*, going one song better than The Magnetic Fields *69 Love Songs*, that would indeed include seventy songs and match *Know Your Enemy* in its messy ambition. Of course it was too good to be true, but nonetheless the band were clearly in an ambitious mood. When the announcement came that the Manic Street Preachers would release, not just one record, but two within the same year, interest (including my own) in the band sky-rocketed. The mostly acoustic and sombre *Rewind the Film* was released in October 2013. The first track to be previewed shared the album's title, a six-minute slow burner with shades of Ennio Morricone guitar. The song also featured the dulcet tones of singer/songwriter Richard Hawley leading the track. James Dean Bradfield's vocals didn't make an appearance until after the three-minute mark. The song itself was a tender lament to youthful nostalgia, old records, faded films and loving books. Like This Is Yesterday, The Everlasting and Indian Summer, the song, and in respect, the album's title and theme, addressed the longing for youth in the midst of middle age or for the 'Whole days throwing sticks into streams' as *The Holy Bible*'s Die In The Summertime explained.

Though not an official single, the video that accompanied the song was a short film by Welsh filmmaker Kieran Evans

REWIND
THE FILM

"Take this, it's yours."
Rewind The Film record sleeve

that centred on a rundown working men's club in the Welsh valleys, and followed the old geezer who tends to the club's upkeep. The official singles from the album, Show Me The Wonder and Anthem For A Lost Cause returned to the same theme of nostalgia, Welsh identity and the trade union working class culture of the Valleys. The promotional video for the brassy Show Me The Wonder harked back to the heyday of the working men's club of the late 1970s and featured the band in fetching leather jackets and fake sideburns (and Moore wearing a moustache) performing the song for the gathered audience. The video for Anthem For A Lost Cause saw the band celebrate women's involvement in the 1984 miners' strike, and what Kieran Evans called:

... a modern British civil war. The heroic battle that wives of miners and the women's support groups waged against an oppressive state hell bent on destroying their communities should be an inspiration to all. They represented the very essence of true socialist principles; collectivising and organising themselves not only to protest against the huge injustice they suffered at the hands of Thatcher but also to feed, clothe and support their fellow workers and their families. In some small way we wanted to bring a sense of this history to the promo and shine a light on the heroic women who took on Thatcher and her thugs.[62]

The working class fury that the band had failed to fully translate on the song S.Y.M.M. became far more apparent on *Rewind the Film*'s final track, 30 Year War, a scathing attack on modern neoliberalism as 'the longest running joke in history' and the 'endless parade of old Etonian scum' who for decades have lined the front benches of parliament. In an essay for the band's 'Journal' page of their website, Richard King commended the song:

> In reawakening and confronting the demons of class rage in middle age there is [a] form of redemption, even if the scars of the Miners' Strike are slower to heal than the scars of the coal seam. Thirty years on, the enduring legacy of Thatcherism in Wales is that we still attempt to live in a society that her regime insisted was nothing more than an article of bad faith.[63]

In the context of *Rewind the Film*'s overall delicate sombreness and personal reflection, 30 Year War was a timely reminder of the band's political roots and still simmering working class rage.

The Manic Street Preachers may have no longer spoken so bluntly of socialism and protest. Their latest songs basked in their own sense of nostalgia and sense of what hope, magic and tragedy their past held, but also the history of the places they came from. Nevertheless, by shaping their audio and visual aesthetics to look back on themselves, their class, and their cultural/personal history, it brilliantly reminded the listener of what a remarkable band they have always been, and thus it reminds us what they have always stood for: a quiet, dignified and classical socialist stance.

BUT IN THE FIELD OF RECORD SALES, JAMES DEAN Bradfield's comments to *Ultimate Guitar* magazine were telling of a band that were now entrusted with producing quality recordings and observing their distinguished position as rock music elders.

> We wanted to know we could sell 100,000 records — 50,000 of each of these two records in one year — and we did. It's a strange thing to bring up but I think you've got to be aware of the world we live in now commercially. You can't spend forever in the studio and spend as much money as you want. You've got to work within the framework of this savage commercial landscape we live in now.[64]

The band's acknowledgement of the 'savage commercial landscape' and their place in it was telling of the industry changes that had occurred over the past decade and a half with the rise of internet downloads and piracy. Even a well-established band such as the Manic Street Preachers had to answer to their paymasters.

*Futurology*, the band's twelfth record, offered a reinterpretation, and whilst the band had often embraced American pop cultural influences in the past, on *Futurology* they now turned to European art, music, politics and architecture for inspiration. James Dean Bradfield explained: 'We started touring mainland Europe in late '91 so obviously we've seen Belfast change in front of our eyes, we've seen Berlin change unbelievably and parts of Belgium... every city in Britain we've seen change.'[65] The change implied is optimistic. Indeed, krautrock and Kraftwerk impose a huge influence on the sound of the record's first single, Walk Me To The Bridge. This convergence of European art and music in conjunction with their history was explained by Bradfield in the *NME*:

"Europäischer himmel, Europäischer wünsche." Futurology record sleeve

> There are not many things that unite Europe but there are two things. It's a post-war civility and there's a complication whenever you cross a border, whether it's Germany and Austria or England and Wales. There are connections there, whether it be art movements that knew nothing of each other.[66]

Nicky Wire went on to point out the differences between *Futurology* and *Rewind the Film*.

> There's an overriding concept behind *Futurology* which is to express all the inspiration we get from travel, music and art — all those ideas, do that in a positive way. *Rewind the Film* was a harrowing forty-five-year-old looking in the mirror, lyrically. *Futurology* was very much an album of ideas.[67]

It was a triumph that Manic Street Preachers could still generate new ideas and still keep true to their original sound and experience. With *Rewind the Film* and *Futurology* they had at last found that balance. The record even contained a criticism of the band's Cuban escapades. On the song, The Next Jet To Leave Moscow, the band explained that their politics are now that of an 'old jaded commie'. The Cuba concert is referenced with the author stating 'I bet you felt proud, you silly little fucker'.

BUT COULD *FUTUROLOGY* ALSO BE A SIGN LIKE *KNOW YOUR Enemy* that the band was out of step with the times, or reacting against the popular (or populist) sentiments, at least politically speaking. In May 2013, the British Conservative Party, then in a government coalition with the Liberal Democrats, published a draft EU Referendum bill and outlined their plans for renegotiation and then a public vote on membership of European Union if the party returned to power after the general election in May 2015. The bill was a direct appeasement to the anti-European wing of the party, who threatened to flock to Nigel Farage's United Kingdom Independence Party (UKIP) if a vote wasn't put forward. The Conservatives won a slim majority in the May 2015 election, meaning the party had the mandate to push forward the EU Referendum bill, or Brexit, as the referendum became known in the media. The farcical In/Out campaign pitted ally against ally, and saw sworn ideological enemies share the same stage in an attempt to persuade the public to leave or remain members of the EU. Both camps made bold and untrue statements about the UK's current membership conditions, and what a post-Brexit Britain would look like. On 23 June 2016 the British public voted by 51.9% to leave the European Union. It was seen as a massive blow to progressive politics and led to the resignation of British Prime Minister David Cameron.

A month before the Brexit vote, Manic Street Preachers released Together Stronger (C'mon Wales), the official Wales EURO 2016 song. It was the first time in over half a century that the Welsh football squad had made it to a major football tournament. Manic Street Preachers were in the midst of openly celebrating European values, art, engineering and sport. Tracks from *Futurology* such as the instrumental Dreaming A City (Hughesovka), which referred to John Hughes, the Welsh engineer, businessman and founder of the Ukrainian city of Donetsk. The song Europa Geht Durch Mich ('Europe Passes Through Me') was a duet with German actress Nina Hoss who sung her lines in her native German, whilst Walk Me To The Bridge was written during a journey across the Oresund Bridge, the five-mile construction that connects Sweden and Denmark. Together Stronger (C'mon Wales), whilst a song of Welsh pride, was also a backhanded defiant slogan of comradeship with Europe. Much like they did with *Know Your Enemy* and the endorsement of socialist values in an age of neoliberalism, Manic Street Preachers pushed European values at a time of Euro-scepticism.

# POSTSCRIPT

WHEN ASKED IN 2009 BY THE WEBSITE *DROWNED IN Sound* if he'd ever consider a *Holy Bible* revue tour Nicky Wire responded: 'No. When we're finished and we need the money...! But no, it's just the sign, really, that you don't matter — that you've become nostalgic.'[68] Manic Street Preachers had so far not run out of good ideas, in fact their latest output indicated they were in the throes of a creative rainy season. Nostalgia for the band's past might have played a part in *Send Away the Tigers*, *Postcards From a Young Man* and *Journal for Plague Lovers*, but *Rewind the Film* and *Futurology* had pointed to some exciting prospects for the band's future that didn't rely on nostalgia, at least not in sound.

It was no surprise the band would want to celebrate a twentieth anniversary of *The Holy Bible*, after all, the record is a milestone not just of the band's career but of late twentieth-century recorded music. Yet with creative output currently in overdrive, an understated memoriam might have been expected. Instead, the twentieth anniversary of *The Holy Bible* was a blowout and a raucous success at that. Manic Street Preachers played a number of concerts in the UK and Europe in which the record was played live and in chronological order and even managed to sell out decent sized venues in the ever-elusive North American market. This celebration was concluded with a triumphant live rendition of the record at

Cardiff Castle. The band even donned the mismatched military uniforms (though this time they were spanking new), evoking the militaristic aesthetics of the *Bible* era. In the second half of the Cardiff show the band changed to more respectful attire and charged through a hit-packed second half. However, the situation of today's Manic Street Preachers is a very different beast. The band's *re*-re-release of *The Holy Bible* after a succession of hugely successful records and a newfound appreciation from fans and critics alike shows that an album so full of contempt and utter bile can now be revisited and reframed in a theatrical light. The twentieth anniversary celebration diffuses the original and now can be reproached as an exercise in nostalgia for the music, a lessening of the radical politics, and makes the military attire less a uniform, more a costume.

But the nostalgia trip didn't end, or in some respects even begin with *The Holy Bible*. *Generation Terrorists*, the band's barnstorming debut was the subject of a twentieth anniversary treatment in 2012. A repackaging of the record was issued containing a bonus DVD of music videos, television appearances, and interviews. *Everything Must Go* was also subject to a twentieth anniversary revisit. The record was reissued, concerts arranged and even a film was commissioned to commemorate the era in which Manic Street Preachers redefined themselves in the dying years of Britpop. As I write this, *Send Away the Tigers*, the record that saved the band from plummeting to obscurity by re-institutionalizing the glitter and bang of the band's past, is scheduled for a tenth anniversary edition and the reviews are even better than first time around.

Even with the band's desire in place to recapitalize on past glories, it's hard to believe that there will be forthcoming in

2021 a twentieth anniversary edition of *Know Your Enemy*. It is very unlikely the band will jet back over to Cuba for a commemorative concert and embrace Raul Castro. Perhaps this is wise. Despite its obvious faults, the record *Know Your Enemy* and the period of the band's career discussed at length in this book felt, to a degree, dangerous, like it would all fall apart at any moment. A band at the height of its success and powers, playing anthem after anthem in stadia designed to absorb football chants, tossed it all aside and released an album that sounded like a joker's mixtape, gave out free hugs to socialist dictators, and taunted other bands in the music press for not having the guts to follow through. The band felt alive, schizophrenic for sure, but open to any possibility. Would any band want to revisit and commemorate such a weird schism?

For the newer fans of Manic Street Preachers, those of us who latched on during the mid-to-late nineties, the answer might be *yes*. *Know Your Enemy* is in many ways our *Holy Bible*. The one time we have in living memory when the band was as confrontational and as uncompromising as they were on that monolithic record. At the time it was actually hard being a fan of the band because you had to explain away Miss Europa Disco Dancer as fun experimentation, or try to justify Nicky Wire's singing voice by citing Lou Reed and Mark E. Smith as predecessors of tuneless vocal performance. It all felt relevant and somehow innovative. Yet, maybe for the reasons stated above, a retrospective of *Know Your Enemy* might go some way to diffuse and dilute the experience somewhat.

And this is my truth (tell me yours), the great contradiction of being a Manic Street Preachers fan, is that one expects the grand gestures and the epic failures. Personally, I want the schizophrenia of an album like *Know Your Enemy* to keep me engaged and thirsty for those cultural footnotes that are so utterly important. Being a fan of Manic Street Preachers today is an incredibly easy thing. They now make consistently great records, aural adventures in the classic sense, with seemingly no room for failure or catastrophe. They pore over their back catalogue, retuning and reviving their past as it gets further away. They haven't become boring or irrelevant, because a band like the Manic Street Preachers will never *be* boring or irrelevant. Yet it feels like they have lost the ramshackle sense of making it up as they go along, the miscalculations that made them so interesting in the first place. Even now what might have been deemed their greatest failure, *The Holy Bible*, a commercial disaster at the time of release, and one that very nearly destroyed the band, has now been shaped into their greatest success and worthy of repeated retrospection.

So what am I trying to say? That the Manic Street Preachers have failed? In a way, yes. They failed at their own ambitions. There was never going to be a clear path towards the kind of band they set out to be and maintain such a position. Failure was always their destiny, because the icons and ideologies they identified with were failures also. We are all guilty of wanting to change the world when we're young. We think our actions will produce some profound movement that will reshape our social consciousness. The Manic Street Preachers wanted to change the world when they first launched themselves at the world. Despite no credible evidence that rock 'n' roll could do this, they persisted anyway. And we as fans placed our faith in them. But, did we place in them too much faith? I certainly did. My insistence in them remaining some stubborn firebrand political entity as they embraced ageing sensibilities of content, marriage, success, parenthood, the throes of daily life was to delay, or in some cases cease any activism or idea of political change I could enact, or new knowledge I could gain. For years I was convinced that Manic Street Preachers were absolutely righteous, so when they played *Strictly Come Dancing* or re-released a bunch of old records and toured them in the guise of a revival act I felt a sense of betrayal usually reserved for a deceitful lover. I realised only fairly recently (perhaps as I entered my own version of middle age, marriage and parenthood) that Manic Street Preachers never needed to change the world, they only ever needed to change people. Their entire meaning was to educate, entertain and offer alternative viewpoints, then let us do the hard work of actually changing things. Through the songs, the record artwork, the writers, artists, thinkers we've seen quoted, the live shows we've attended, and the acts of artistry the band have engaged us in, it is we who have done great things with our lives. Anybody reading this book knows that the band drove you to where you are. The work is far from done

The intention of this book was to make a positive case for *Know Your Enemy*, celebrate the record's victories and admit its flaws yet present them in a way that places them in the context that rock 'n' roll requires mistakes and mishaps in order to be relevant, and show that new avenues can be explored regardless if all that is found is a dead end. If the case has been adequately made, then hopefully a re-listen to *Know Your Enemy* and its surrounding era will reveal it as one of the Manic Street Preachers most accomplished recordings. As the opening line of the record suggests: 'Show me wonder.'

# ACKNOWLEDGEMENTS

MY MAIN THANKS MUST GO TO MY WIFE JAMIE FOR HER continued and constructive support in this, and many other writing projects.

Without Nicky, Sean, James and Richey I may never have written a single word, or perhaps never even read a significant one. The band introduced me and guided me towards culture, language, literature, music, sports, film, politics and people a working class lad from the outskirts of Leicester would have never come across. My eternal gratitude to the Manic Street Preachers themselves.

There have been strange moments and fleeting encounters with fans of the Manic Street Preachers which continue to linger in my memory. On dancefloors, in bus terminals, airports, or walking down winding long roads in long forgotten towns we found moments of recognition and acknowledgement of the fact we loved the Manics.

Whilst researching this project the following archives and fansites were indispensible: Manic Street Mania, Forever Delayed, Terrible Beauty, MSPedia and Hello It's Us Again, and Andrew Johnson's Critical Discography. The enthusiasm for maintaining the archives of Manic history and fandom is commendable.

The following friends, colleagues and acquaintances will always have my thanks: Andrew Jury, Dipesh Patel, Mariam

Ashraf, Hannah Lenagh-Snow, Clare Hardy, Lesley Hammond, Jackie Jarrett, Joanne Lalonde, Greg Haver, Denise Enck, Dan Taylor, Daniel Bristow, Alfie Bown, David Kerekes and the team at Headpress, Tim Carter, David and Kate Gandy, Dean Gandy, David Wright, Signe Blixt Wright, Mark D, Gareth W, Lizzie, The Smiths: Michael, Samantha, Lucas, Archie. Huge thank you to the immensely talented Rebecca Carter @thewritesigns for the cover design of this book.

My family: Jamie, Hayden, Isla, Mum, Dad, Joanne, Libby Evie, Brian, Gail, Ross, Kara, Seamus and Stanley.

# NOTES

1   Lindsey, C (2015, March 7). Rank Your Albums: James Dean
    Bradfield Rates Manic Street Preachers' 12 Albums. *Noisey*.
    Retrieved May 20, 2017. https://noisey.vice.com/en_ca/
    article/6azen4/rank-your-records-manic-street-preachers
2   Ibid.
3   Johns. S (2007, January 11) Notes on the miners strike, 1984–1985.
    *Libcom.org.* Retrieved May 15, 2017. https://libcom.org/library/
    notes-on-the-miners-strike-1984-1985
4   Rosen, S (2015, March 26). Sometimes You Need Some Creative
    Failure to Spur You On. *Ultimate Guitar.* Retrieved April 25, 2017.
    https://www.ultimate-guitar.com/news/interviews/manic_street_
    preachers_james_dean_bradfield_sometimes_you_need_some_
    creative_failure_to_spur_you_on.html
5   Ibid.
6   Price, S. (2008, September 14). A Heavenly Body Of Work — Part
    One. *The Quietus*. Retrieved November 10, 2015. http://thequietus.
    com/articles/00417-manic-street-preachers-a-heavenly-body-of-
    work
7   Hall, M. J. (2014, October 24). Q&A Manic Street Preachers James
    Dean Bradfield on 20 years of Generation Terrorists & more.
    *Q Magazine*. Retrieved November 10, 2016, from http://www.
    qthemusic.com/579/qa-manic-street-preachers-james-dean-
    bradfield-20-years-generation-terrorists/
8   Schurr, M. (2015, April 15) Talking "Method" Recording and
    Youthful Delusions with the Manic Street Preachers. *Pop
    Matters*. Retrieved April 10, 2017. http://www.popmatters.

com/feature/192284-talking-method-recording-and-youthful-delusions-with-manic-street-pr/)/

9    Mackey, E. (2009, May 14) Manic Street Preachers Interview Part Two — 'Therapy Is Bullshit, Talking Never Makes You Feel Good'. *NME*. Retrieved May 13, 2017. http://www.nme.com/blogs/nme-blogs/manic-street-preachers-interview-part-two-therapy-is-bullshit-talking-never-makes-you-feel-good-47462#g2zr96yymmK3r27V.99)

10   NME. (1998, July 28) Police Chief Slams Manics Lyrics. *NME*. Retrieved April 6, 2015. http://www.nme.com/news/music/manic-street-preachers-330-1386497#KzPS1jKcuWq4BpiZ.99

11   Lynskey, D. (2001, March) A Redesign for Life. *Q Magazine*. Retrieved April 6, 2017. http://www.foreverdelayed.org.uk/msppedia/images/3/30/Q2001_%284%29.jpg

12   NME. (2000, May 10) Raw Sixth from the Manics. *NME*. Retrieved April 5, 2017 http://www.nme.com/news/music/manic-street-preachers-359-1391908

13   Gibbons, F. (1999, July 24). Red rockers wage battle of Portaloo. Retrieved August 25, 2015,. https://www.theguardian.com/uk/1999/jul/24/fiachragibbons

14   Ibid.

15   Ibid.

16   Lynskey, D. (2001, March) A Redesign for Life. *Q Magazine*. Retrieved April 6, 2017. http://www.foreverdelayed.org.uk/msppedia/images/3/30/Q2001_%284%29.jpg

17   Tzu, S (2002) *The Art of War*. London: Dover Publications. Page 51

18   Leslie, D. (2006, October 15). Incendiary Interviews James Dean Bradfield. Retrieved March 16, 2015. http://www.incendiarymag.com/interviews/manicstreetpreachers/incendiary_interviews_james_dean_bradfield

19   Lynskey, D. (2001, March) A Redesign for Life. *Q Magazine*. Retrieved April 6, 2017. http://www.foreverdelayed.org.uk/msppedia/images/3/30/Q2001_%284%29.jpg

20   ibid.

21  Price, S. (2001, March 02). Our Manics in Havana. *The Guardian*. Retrieved November 15, 2016. https://www.theguardian.com/friday_review/story/0,3605,444837,00.html%2013/8/2015

22  Segal, V. (2005, September 12). Manic Street Preachers : Know Your Enemy. Retrieved August 6, 2015, from http://www.nme.com/reviews/album/reviews-nme-4233

23  Quantick, D. (2014, July 2). Manic Street Preachers: There's just so much hate within this band. Why are we still like this? Retrieved August 13, 2015. http://www.uncut.co.uk/features/manic-street-preachers-there-s-just-so-much-hate-within-this-band-why-are-we-still-like-this-6910#oh4RMcUCShyAYuDH.99.

24  Corbett, A. (2001, November 15). A Design For Values. Retrieved June 26, 2015, from http://www.foreverdelayed.org.uk/msppedia/index.php?title=A_Design_For_Values_-_Pop_Culture_Press,_15th_November_2001

25  Griffiths, D. (2004). *OK computer*. New York: Continuum. Page. 19

26  Interview: Manic Street Preachers, *Muse*. (2001, March 09). Retrieved November 10, 2015, from http://www.foreverdelayed.org.uk/msppedia/index.php?title=Interview:_Manic_Street_Preachers,_Muse,_9th_March_2001

27  Segal, V. (2005, September 12). Manic Street Preachers : Know Your Enemy. Retrieved August 6, 2015, http://www.nme.com/reviews/album/reviews-nme-4233

28  Escalona, A. (2012, May 23). 75 years of Picasso's Guernica: An Inconvenient Masterpiece. Retrieved August 16, 2015, from http://www.huffingtonpost.com/alejandro-escalona/75-years-of-picassos-guernica-_b_1538776.html

29  Lindsey, C (2015, March 7). Rank Your Albums: James Dean Bradfield Rates Manic Street Preachers' 12 Albums. *Noisey*. Retrieved May 20, 2017. https://noisey.vice.com/en_ca/article/6azen4/rank-your-records-manic-street-preachers

30  Gibbs, G. (1999, May 26). We won't play for the royals, say manic street preachers. *The Guardian*. Retrieved December 11, 2015. https://www.theguardian.com/uk/1999/may/26/monarchy.

geoffreygibbs

31  Price, S. (2001, March 02). Our Manics in Havana. *The Guardian*. Retrieved August 12, 2015 https://www.theguardian.com/friday_review/story/0,3605,444837,00.html

32  Reid, B. (2001, March 19). Manic Street Preachers: Know Your Enemy | 7.5. *Pitchfork*. Retrieved August 17, 2015. http://pitchfork.com/reviews/albums/5072-know-your-enemy/

33  NME. (1998) Radio Hades. *NME*. Retrieved March 23, 2017 http://www.nme.com/reviews/album/reviews-nme-151

34  Price, S. (2001, March 02). Our Manics in Havana. *The Guardian*. Retrieved August 12, 2015. https://www.theguardian.com/friday_review/story/0,3605,444837,00.html

35  Ibid.

36  Ibid.

37  Liddell, M. (2001, July 8). Overcoming Manic depression. *Japan Times*. Retrieved November 11, 2015, http://www.japantimes.co.jp/culture/2001/07/08/music/overcoming-manic-depression-2/

38  Trousse, S. T. (2012, August 09). An audience with... Manic street preachers' Nicky Wire. *Uncut Magazine*. Retrieved June 15, 2015. http://www.uncut.co.uk/features/an-audience-with-manic-street-preachers-nicky-wire-20207

39  Ibid.

40  Jeffries, S. (2016.December 10). AA Gill Obituary. *The Guardian*. Accessed April 4, 2017. https://www.theguardian.com/media/2016/dec/10/aa-gill-obituary.

41  Sony. (2008, June 01). Manic Street Preachers Biographie. Retrieved May 10, 2015, from Sony music entertainment, https://www.sonymusic.ch/kuenstler/manic-street-preachers

42  Beaumont, M. (2005, September 12). Manic street preachers: Forever delayed. *NME* Retrieved July 29, 2015. *NME*. http://www.nme.com/reviews/album/reviews-nme-6788

43  Parkes, T. (2014, December 9) There Are No Horizons: The Holy Bible At 20, By Taylor Parkes. The Quietus. Retrieved May 29, 2017.

http://thequietus.com/articles/16863-manic-street-preachers-holy-bible-20

44    Reid, B. (2001, March 19). Manic street preachers: Know your enemy. *Pitchfork.* Retrieved May 17, 2015. http://pitchfork.com/reviews/albums/5072-know-your-enemy/

45    Lynskey, D. (2004, October 1). Not so manic now. *The Guardian.* Retrieved June 2, 2016. https://www.theguardian.com/music/2004/oct/01/2

46    Price, S. (2004, October 23) Manic Street Preachers: Sublime and Ridiculous. *The Independent.* Retrieved May 18, 2017. http://www.independent.co.uk/arts-entertainment/music/features/manic-street-preachers-sublime-and-ridiculous-545030.html

47    Interview with author

48    Reed, M. (2006, September 30). NICKY WIRE "I killed the Zeitgeist." Retrieved April 14, 2015,. http://www.thefinalword.co.uk/content/view/508/25/

49    Trousse, S. T. (2012, August 09). An audience with... Manic street preachers' Nicky Wire. *Uncut Magazine.* Retrieved June 15, 2015. http://www.uncut.co.uk/features/an-audience-with-manic-street-preachers-nicky-wire-20207

50    Interview with author

51    Nicholson, B. (2007) Manic Street Preachers: Send Away the Tigers. *NME.* Retrieved July 4, 2017. http://www.nme.com/reviews/album/reviews-manic-street-preachers-8498

52    Keefe, M. (2007, July 22) Manic Street Preachers: Send Away the Tigers. *Pop Matters.* Retrieved June 27, 2017. http://www.popmatters.com/review/manic-street-preachers-send-away-the-tigers/

53    Petridis, A. (2009, May 08). This Album Could Seriously Damage Us. *The Guardian.* Retrieved November 11, 2016. http://www.foreverdelayed.org.uk/msppedia/index.php?title=%27This_Album_Could_Seriously_Damage_Us%27_-_The_Guardian,_8th_May_2009

54    Ibid.

55    Ibid.

56  Price, K. (2010, September 14). Manics rage against the machine on 10th album. Retrieved June 22, 2015,. Wales Online, http://www.walesonline.co.uk/lifestyle/showbiz/manics-rage-against-machine-10th-1897952

57  Fullerton, J. (2010, June 1). Manic street preachers announce UK tour and new album details. Retrieved February 12, 2015, from *NME*, http://www.nme.com/news/music/manic-street-preachers-127-1294769

58  Nissim, M. (2016, November 14). Ex-GN'R bassist features on new Manics LP. Retrieved March 03, 2015, from Digital Spy, http://www.digitalspy.com/music/news/a223960/ex-gnr-bassist-features-on-new-manics-lp/

59  Stokes, P. (2010, September 17). Manic street preachers Nicky Wire: "Nick Clegg reminds me of David Brent." *NME*. Retrieved April 11, 2015. http://www.nme.com/news/music/manic-street-preachers-111-1299595

60  Wilkinson, M. (2011, February 4). Nicky Wire "gutted" when Manics missed top 40 for first time since 1991. *NME*. Retrieved April 05, 2015. http://www.nme.com/news/music/manic-street-preachers-119-1287060

61  Grundy, G. (2011, October 30). Nicky Wire: "An artist? I'm a Polaroid freak." *The Guardian*. Retrieved April 7, 2015. https://www.theguardian.com/music/2011/oct/30/manic-street-wire-photographs-book

62  Tuffrey, L. T. (2013, October 13). WATCH: New manic street preachers video. Retrieved May 23, 2015, from *The Quietus*. http://thequietus.com/articles/13574-manic-street-preachers-anthem-for-a-lost-cause-video-2

63  King, R. (2013, October 10). We may write in English but our truth remains in wales. Retrieved June 11, 2015, from Manicstreetpreachers.com, https://www.manicstreetpreachers.com/journal/we-may-write-english-our-truth-remains-wales/

64  Rosen, S. R. (2015, March 26). Manic street preachers' James Dean Bradfield: "Sometimes you need some creative failure to spur you

on" *Ultimate Guitar*. Retrieved December 03, 2015. Ultimate Guitar, https://www.ultimate-guitar.com/news/interviews/manic_street_ preachers_james_dean_bradfield_sometimes_you_need_some_ creative_failure_to_spur_you_on.html

65   GQ. (2014, July 14) GQ&A with James Dean Bradfield. *GQ* magazine. Retrieved October 13, 2016. http://www.foreverdelayed.org.uk/ msppedia/index.php?title=GQ%26A_With_James_Dean_Bradfield_-_ GQ,_14th_July_2014

66   Daly, R. (2014, July 10). Manic street preachers' Nicky Wire: "Futurology" is one of our most optimistic records'. Retrieved May 02, 2015, from *NME*, http://www.nme.com/news/music/manic-street-preachers-45-1237760

67   Ibid.

68   AD, C. (2009, June 19). Nicky Wire on the press, Shirley Bassey, and the future of Manic Street Preachers. Retrieved April 07, 2015, from *Drowned in Sound*, http://drownedinsound.com/ in_depth/4137164-nicky-wire-on-the-press-shirley-bassey-and-the-future-of-the-manic-street-preachers—part-three

**A HEADPRESS BOOK**
**First published by Headpress in 2018**

{e} headoffice@headpress.com

**RIFFS & MEANING**
**Manic Street Preachers and *Know Your Enemy***

A CIP catalogue record for this book is available from
the British Library

ISBN 978-1-909394-56-8 (paperback)
ISBN 978-1-909394-57-5 (ebook)
NO-ISBN (hardback)

Headpress. The gospel according to unpopular culture.

NO ISBN special edition hardbacks and other items
are available exclusively from Headpress

HEADPRESS.COM